REFLECTIONS

of my life living with Cerebral Palsy

Julia Mitchell

First published in the United Kingdom in 2016 by
Julia Mitchell

ISBN 978-0-955996-71-9

Image Jumbulance used with kind permission from ACROSS
(www.across.org.uk)

This book is dedicated to my closest friend, John Ryan,
who died on the 23rd July 2015.

I would like to thank Helen Redding for typing this book on the computer from the beginning until 2013, and checking my English.

My thanks for these people who have given me help when I required it:

John Ryan
Joanne Tomsett
Wayne Kinge
Timothy Wilmot
Gill Chandler

Tim became unwell in September 2015 and did not return to work. He is going to retire in January 2016. Thank you for being my PA, for supporting me, for the laughter we had together and for reading books to me, including the Bible.

Thanks to Harriet Evans for copy-editing, Adrian Sysum for the book design and Rachel Woodman for the cover design.

I would like to thank Frank Keen for proof reading and ideas to improve the book.

About the Book

I was born with cerebral palsy. I started to write poetry in the seventies as a way of releasing my feelings about life. In 2001, I started again writing about my relationship with God and the Church. About this time I started to lose my sight and ended up a wheelchair user and my life was turned upside down. I began to write poems on my everyday life and my feelings about my increased disability. Some are about me, my carers and other subjects.

Contents

Introduction

I started to write poetry during the 1970s in my twenties. I was quite nervous and conscious of my speech, especially when it came to words that I couldn't say properly. I was very good at hiding my true feelings. I would find it hard to express myself to those around me. I still get a lump in my throat over good news or anything sad. Writing poetry is another way to get it off my chest instead of letting it boil up inside me.

During the next fifteen years, I didn't do as much as I would have liked to do as I was studying for my Diploma in Health and Wellbeing and then a degree in Art with the Open University, for the RSA Counselling Skills certificate, for the Sports Leadership certificate and for my City & Guilds 730 teaching certificate in Adult Education.

I wasn't prompted to write any more poetry until 2001, when I heard excerpts from The Other Side of the Dale by Gervase Phinn on the radio. I enjoyed it so much that I wanted to go and buy the book and get John to read it all to me.

Gervase Phinn passionately believes that everyone, especially children, should write poetry to increase their vocabulary and use their imagination and ideas. I suppose this is what started me thinking when I had to spend more time on my own at home, as I could no longer go out on my own. My cataract was growing and I already had glaucoma. Apart from listening to the radio, I did have a lot of time on my hands to think and to write.

Most of my poetry seems to lean towards religion, carers and related subjects. The reason why is that I think the Church has got a lot to learn about people with disabilities. The feelings I have as a Christian with disabilities who worships a loving God have often troubled me. There can also be friction between a carer and a disabled person. I have also felt that churches have got a long way to go to encourage people with disabilities to join.

Sometimes I might get two ideas on the same day and I may be working on one poem, then I go back to finish the other poem.

I hope you find these poems inspiring and interesting and that they will encourage you to think about your faith. If you are an able-bodied person, I hope that these poems will help you to understand and be aware of the difficulties of disabled people within the Church and life around a disabled person.

There are two themes which are repeated again and again in my poems:

A.   God knows my heart.

B.   God knows the answer.

I believe that family and friends do know you but God knows you even more. God does know the answer to every situation we go through. Jesus understands everything about suffering.

Chapter One

It came as a surprise to me, when looking back over my poetry, how much my life had changed since finding Allerford Church, King's Church and healing.

I feel that I have been led by the Holy Spirit to write poems about these churches and about my healing. I did not plan to write these poems, and it is only when I look back through the poems that I realise that God was leading me to begin a special journey in my life.

As you read through the poetry, I can share with you my feelings on how I found the Church and God, and found a greater awareness of other people around me.

Some of my experiences with the Church have not always been positive ones. But now I am a lot older, I can appreciate that the blame did not always lie with other people.

God has shown me the path he wants me to take, and I had to go through these experiences to learn.

In this section there was one church where a member did upset me but, at the time, I wasn't strong enough to stand up for myself. She thought she knew the cause of my cerebral palsy – yet I knew the answer to how I was born with cerebral palsy.

One evening, I went home from my house group crying, all because someone said I was self-centred. I didn't know how to deal with that one.

Someone said that the umbilical cord got caught round my neck, stopping some of the oxygen reaching my brain.

Another said I was born with a disability because of my parents' sins. I knew this wasn't true because of John chapter 9.

A good few years later, a Christian friend of mine told me my life would be turned upside down, and that person was right.

Section A

This is where I have chosen some of my early poems that I wrote during the 1970s and 1980s. There are a few of these early poems in other parts of the book.

A GREAT FRIEND

" I wrote this poem in the seventies for someone, but now I can't remember the person's name. "

I have a great friend,
Whom I have known for years.
We have been good to each other,
As we are good friends.

When I'm feeling sad and lonely,
I go to see this friend of mine.
We sit down for hours,
Talking of all the things we've done,
Then we start to laugh.
That is how we go about it,
My friend and I.

When I need help
To do the things I cannot do,
I go and see my friend,
And he or she will do it for me.
Whether they do it just to keep me quiet,
Or whether they do it because they feel they have to,
I try to think of it this way:
I am lucky to have them,
My friends and I,
As we do get on well together;
Where would I be without them?

21st October 1976

The Ghost House

" This poem came to me after reading Great Expectations by Charles Dickens. "

There is an old house
Which has been burnt by fire.
I walk inside to have a look,
Then I walk in one of the rooms.
Behind the door
I can see a settee.
I move a bit closer
As the room is very dark.
On the settee I can see a young girl.
Her body is covered with dust.
I bend down to have a look
And this is what I see.
Her body is long and thin.
She has a long white dress on.
She has long black hair
Which is covered in dust.
Her face is clear white.
Her eyes are closed.
Her lips are dry.
Her arms are crossed
As if she has been dead for many years.
She is the ghost of the house!

TEA LEAVES

" *This poem was written when I was at Bromley Workshop with Paula. It is no longer there and the members have moved on.*

I saw Paula in the nineties on the Sports Day at Ladywell Day Centre. Twice a year the centre held competitions for different boroughs. Paula was going to college, getting a flat and getting married the following year. "

Tea leaves in a packet, waiting to make a pot of tea.
Many people like it, many people don't,
But when it comes to the tea leaves part at the end
Some people just throw them down the drain,
Some people tell their future,
Some come true and some don't come true,
And now there is a pot of tea waiting for me.

Horror Film

Lying in bed one night
After watching a horror film
When my curtains are wide open
When the light is shining through my window
The light is shining onto my wall
On the wall where the light is
I can see a shadow
I wonder what it is
As I can't see it clearly
But I know it has something to do with the film
As I lie there not moving one part of my body
I can hear my heart beating
As I lie there in the dark and look at the wall
My heart is beating faster and faster
My body is getting hotter and hotter
I slowly get out of bed and close the curtains quickly
As I make my way back to bed
My body is very cold
Then I slowly go to sleep

LYING IN BED

Lying in bed one night
Forgetting to close the curtains
Looking out of the window
Staring at the stars in the sky at twelve midnight
Watching the black clouds coming over
The stars are disappearing behind the clouds
Then I can see the lightning far behind
Getting stronger and deeper
The rain falling against my window
Then the thunder is getting louder and louder
As I lie there wondering what to do
I pull my bedclothes over my head
I can hear the thunder and lightning
And the rain against my window
As I gradually go to sleep.

15th August 1976

Blindness (1)

I close my eyes for a minute or two
Wondering what it is like to be blind
When everything is dark
When I'm in the park
I can't see the green grass or the trees
I can't see the flowers
I can only hear the children playing
When I'm in the street
I can't see the traffic
I can't see the vehicles
That rush by me
I can't see in the shop windows
All their lovely things on show
I can't see the houses
The shapes and sizes
I can't see the people around me
I can't see their faces or their hair styles
And how pretty they look
When I open my eyes
How lucky I am to be able to see
All the things that are around me

20th August 1976

MY SECRET PLACE

I went to visit my secret place.
I haven't been there for years.
I wonder if it has changed
As I make my way down the hill.
Looking around, it doesn't look the same.
I can't remember what is missing.
I begin to think for a while
As I slip my mind back to long ago,
Then I can see nothing is missing.
They are building foundations on my secret place.
I begin to wonder whether I like it.
I can still see the rooftops
But this is not my secret place.
So I take another path
Hoping to end in my secret place.
Looking ahead, I am sure to find it.
After a while, I come to my secret place.
It is really like being in the woods.
There are trees on both sides
With steps going through the middle.
I am really glad they haven't harmed this part.
I decide to praise God,
Which I've never done before.
I sit on a seat for a while
As I'm talking to God.
Slowly I move away from my place
Wondering whether it is still my secret place.
Looking around, don't mind what they did to my secret place.
It looks so lovely, my secret place.

23rd August 1982

Do I Really Want to Marry?

"*This one was written after I had been going out with Gordon for ten years. We never really spoke about marriage. A few years ago, a friend of mine told me that he is married with two children. I wonder how many would think I'm referring to my friend John?*"

Do I really want to marry
This man I'm supposed to love?
Do I really love him?
Does he really love me?
And yet he never shows his love.
I know he isn't a Christian.
There's so much to think about,
All the 'for's and 'against's.
Money isn't the problem.
Housing isn't either.
All the things I ask myself:
Could I bear to live with him?
Have I enough patience for him?
Would I really let myself go
To be what he wants me to be?
It's not only the give and take,
Yet I know all the answers,
But how do I tell him?
As he is so good to me
When I just take him for a friend.

28th March 1983

PRESENTS

Why do I choose to buy my friends presents?
Is it because I wish to show that I love them?
Or is it to show my appreciation
For their kindness and consideration?
I often wonder why I do it.
The part I enjoy is buying the cards,
Finding in them meaning in the words.
You can buy cards for all situations,
Those that portray true feelings
So that my friends can see I care.
This is part of my Christian life.
So that is why I buy my friends presents
                                    8th April 1983

ONE SPRING MORNING

One spring morning
The sun was shining
I went for a walk
Through the woods
I walk through the woods
Slowly and quietly
So that I can hear the birds
I could hear the birds singing
And the trees blowing against other trees
There I was just standing there
Listening to the birds and trees
On my way home from the woods
Looking behind me
As I walked my way home
The woods were far behind me

By the Window

Standing by my bedroom window
Looking over the gardens
I can see a tree moving
Not very far from me
With a light behind it
I can see the outlines of the roofs
And the sky is clear
I can see the sunset
Gradually going down
The stars are shining
As I look round
There's no more to see
As I turn my head away from the window

13th September 1976

AFTERNOON

One afternoon
Walking in the park
I sit on the edge of the bank
Looking down onto the water
As the water flows by
I can see the pattern of the water
As it flows around the stones
And the dry leaves are floating on top
As I look up over to the other side
I can see a whole line of trees
Behind the trees
There is a railway line
As I get up to walk away
I can hear a train coming through
As I walk, I turn my head
And the train is far behind me
And the sound of the train
Is gradually getting softer
As I walk my way through the park

14th September 1976

MONDAY-TO-MONDAY (1)

Monday, I'm feeling great.
Tuesday, I'm feeling tired.
Wednesday, I'm in a mood.
Thursday, I am worried.
Friday, I'm feeling rough.
Saturday, I am ill.
Sunday, I'm getting better.
Monday, I feel great again.
   24th September 1976

ONE RAINY NIGHT

One raining night
Sitting on the edge of my bed
Looking out of the window
I could hear and see the children playing in the rain
Laughing, screaming and shouting about
People walking or running by
Some men had newspapers on their heads to stop them getting wet
Some men were running like mad without anything on their heads
Ladies were running with and without umbrellas
The colours, shapes and sizes of them all
I was amazed that I could not see one alike!
And now the rain has stopped
And everything is nice and quiet once more

A Change

I went to my evening class
Didn't really want to go
Afraid of what might come about
Sure that something would
But what, I could not say
Often I had a sensation
Which I could not understand
Happy when I was in two, three or four
In a crowd I was lost and sad
Sometimes I would wonder off
To find out what was happening
To find out what I am taking in
Slowly I grew aware of myself
Wondering how to overcome
Though I must have known the answer
Myself alone must make the move
No one else can do it for me
But can I let myself go?
Then I began to feel a change
With effort, I was able to talk
I can talk to those I feared
I found the group patience helping me through
Terri, I can turn to for my guidance

20th September 1986

ON MY WAY HOME

On my way home
Thinking about tonight,
Wondering what I can write.
Had a chewing gum to calm me,
Feeling nervous and uneasy
About this peer group
Knowing what my needs are,
Whether I shall go by them,
Would be comfortable if I did.
Whom shall I ask, old or new?
Maybe Joanne and Anne.
Need more time to think.
As they are willing to have me,
Would I be happy with them?
Would they meet my needs?
I think I have decided.
Yes, Johann and Anne it will be.

1st October 1986

COUNSELLING

Wasn't nervous or worried
But was concerned about my body
With aches and pains here and there,
Wondering how am I going to cope?
Controlling my body for speech
Can worry me more than anything else.
Arrived at the college waiting for Anne.
Had a drink to wash my tablets down.
Surprised to see Anne in a collar
As now we are both in the same boat.
Felt as if we didn't care about tonight.
Didn't bother to practise but talked.
Walked to the tutor's room to report.
Reading the aims, my voice went funny.
Felt silly in the 'Hello' game but was good.
Communication – felt shaking but comfortable.
Trying too hard put me off.
Role play was difficult for both of us.
I wandered off in my group of four.
Now it was time to feedback on the whole evening.
Pleased, very surprised at the way I handled it.
Didn't care what the others thought.
Very surprised at what they did say.
Enjoyed it with Anne but glad it was over.

6th November 1986

Section B

Section B is about my journey into Christ and my early experiences of growing up and going to church.

JOURNEY

"I became a Christian in 1980. I was guided by Holy Spirit to write about my journey to Christ."

I made a new friend at Ladywell.
His name is Maurice.
At lunchtime,
A laugh and a chat.
Over time,
I realised there is something in him,
As the weeks went by,
We started talking about God.
It was just something to chat about.
I gave him all my questions on God.
In the Bible, he found most of the answers.
I kept asking more and more.
After months went by,
I committed my life to Jesus.
Maurice and John M gave me a Bible.

Everything looked different,
Then I knew that Jesus was in me.
What a lovely feeling it was,
Though it didn't last long.

I started on my journey with Jesus.
                                    23rd December 2001

Disabled

"*I like to think I got this idea as my mum became disabled later in life.*"

Becoming disabled later in life.
What a terrible experience
For anyone to go through,
Either by accident or natural causes.
What hardship it brings
For the family or loved ones.
It leaves unanswered questions,
Why us or *Why me?*
Who is to blame?
Me, God or the person involved?
Whatever form it takes,
It needs love, care and understanding.
Learning to cope with it
Is another experience,
No matter how traumatic.
It depends on that person;
Whether to go forward or backward,
Depends on who you are.
Making the most of what is left,
In accepting it or not is the key
That will help you through.
Becoming disabled you may find yourself
Doing things you never dreamt of.

26th June 2001

LIFE (1)

"Written before I became a Christian."

The way I see life
Is not the way you see it.
The way I see people
Is like being at war.
The way I see work
Is just a waste of time,
But has to be done.
The way I see music
Is a way to relax.
The way I see nature
Is to show
How patient life can be.
The way I see time,
It just flies by.
The way I see love
Is peaceful and joy.
The way I see death,
I cannot say.
The way I see me
Is what I am
And always shall be.
The way I see you
Is just another person!

12th September 1976

Life (2)

"Written after I became a Christian."

The way I see life
Is to do God's will.
The way I see people,
To be like a family.
The way I see work
Is to work for God.
The way I see music
Is a way to relax.
The way I see nature
Is to show God's beauty.
The way I see time,
To keep me going.
The way I see love
Is to show my care.
The way I see death,
It will be glorious.
The way I see me
Is part of God
And always will be.
The way I see you
Is to show I care.

4th April 1983

DOWNE

I spent a week in Downe.
Didn't really want to go,
Afraid of what might come about,
For I felt sure that something would!
But what, I could not say.
Often I had a sensation
Which I could not understand.
Happy when I was alone with God,
In a crowd I was lost and sad.
Sometimes I would wonder off,
To find God and to be alone,
To talk and to sing my songs to Him.
Slowly I grew aware of myself,
Wondering how to overcome,
Though I must have known the answer.
Myself alone must make the move.
No one else could do it for me.
But could I just let myself go?
Then I began to feel a change.
I could worship God in a crowd.
I could talk to those whom I feared.
I found God's blessing helping me through,
But I must take my next step alone.
I still had to ask for deliverance
From my fear of living and life!
How far would I have to go?
I thought, perhaps my next step to me would be shown.

16th August 1982

Allerford Chapel

"Allerford merged with King's Church. Now they have three buildings. The main one is Catford Hill, then Downham and Lee."

Allerford Chapel,
Modern and pleasant,
Neat and warm,
But church is people, not bricks and mortar.

Not C of E or RC,
Very different for me.
No pews, just chairs,
Modern songs, not ancient hymns.
Hands lifted,
Clapping and dancing,
Yes, it was for me.

Pat's my teacher,
Foundation course,
Discipleship,
Receiving the Spirit,
Healing.
Bible studies.
Pat, a friend for life.

Time went on,
Prophecy and praying for me,
Deliverance from demons,
Deliverance from disability,
My feelings changed,
Frightened.
Pressured.
Frustrated.
Sad and excited,
Awaiting for healing,
That never came.

Had to escape,
Should have spoken out,
Couldn't take any more,
Left the Church.
                    2nd–18th January 2002

KING'S CHURCH (1)

King's Church,
A proper church,
Rows and rows of pews,
An organ with pipes,
My Allerford joining King's as one,
As God advised them.

Went for a while,
To see what it was like.
Felt I needed to.
The membership was larger.
Looking around wondering,
Do I fit in?

On one hand,
I was being blessed there.
On the other hand,
Couldn't let myself go.
Something was holding me back,
Blocking the way,
A gap between them and me.
Didn't mix in.
Should I have done?
Could I have done?

Discussed healing again.
Gave my prophecies to the pastor,
Never got them back.
Didn't bother me
Till now.
Felt hurt as they were for me and others.

I thought, No.
Can't go through this again.
After Mum passed away,
I decided to go.
King's Church is not for me.
I don't fit in.
After all the years it is not for me.
Yet for a long time,
If asked, I still say King's is my church.
22nd January 2000

"
The pastor at the time, Martin A, did apologise to me about healing and didn't want to make the same mistake again."

HEALING (1)

WOW!
How exciting!
Me being healed!
Being like able-bodied people,
Being able to do things.
No more struggling,
No more thinking ahead.

Get up, wash and dress,
Pick up knife, fork and spoon and feed myself.
Pick up pen and write,
Correct a book and read.
Put a plug in and switch on.
Walking, getting on and off buses,
Getting ready for bed.

Concentrating
Tiring
Frustrating
Muscle spasms
Time-consuming

Hang on a minute
This is me
I don't know any different
Learnt to cope from birth

The Church,
Were they thinking of me?
Did they wonder what I felt
Or what I was going through?
Were they thinking of the *Church*?
What fame for them,
More people in church.

Praying, be prayed over
Waiting for healing
Afraid and frightened
Pushed down
Under pressure
Too much, too much
Can't take any more
I gave up
Turned away from church
Away from God?

23rd February 2002

HILDA

"*Hilda remained a good friend until 2014 when she started getting confused and slowly got worse. Stoneleigh took over Downe Bible Week from 1991 to 2001.*"

As long as I can remember
Hilda lived in our road
She went to Allerford Chapel
In our house group
'Hello,' was all we said
But on Mondays
We met with her neighbours, Charles and Doreen
For a chat and a laugh
To share each other's news
To have a prayer time

Hilda started visiting Mum
For a chat
To exchange news
They became good friends
Mum died in '96
Hilda asked me to visit her
So Saturday afternoon it was
We eat and drink
We chat and laugh
Study the Bible and prayer
Our friendship grew
Went to Stoneleigh together
Our friendship really took off
I need her more and more

As the weeks went by
My legs and blindness got worse
Hilda became my special friend
Gives me support when I'm down
Understands John's feeling
As she does mine
Little jobs that I can't do
Then when I met her
She would give me her time no matter what
What more could I ask for?

Looking back over this, I can see how God works in our lives
August 2002

What Is Life?

What is life?
You are born with nothing
You die with nothing
Your upbringing and education
Decide who you are going to be
Three things we all do
Eat, work and sleep
We eat to live
We work to pay our way
For those who can – live comfortably
For those who can't – struggle
We sleep a quarter of our life
So what is life?
Is life what you make it?
God has given you a choice
To follow Him or go your own way
To go your way –
No hope, no future
To follow Christ –
Hope and a future

23rd July 2001

WCCI

There is a small church,
Meets in a community centre
Quite close to John's flat.
I thought I'd give it a try.
Was thinking of moving this way.
Didn't think much of it – urk.

God found me a place,
A bungalow I couldn't refuse.
I didn't expect this,
Just perfect.
That church is at the back.
I can't walk without holding an arm.
This church is ideal.

OK, Lord, You win.
You want me to go to that church again.
I go with an open mind
Hoping I won't like it!
Graham, the new leader, makes me feel welcome.
Each Sunday, if he's there and free
He will pop over to say 'Hello.'
Other leaders and members are the same.
I can be myself without any worries.
They accept me as a person, not as an object.
I still get a few ups and downs
But don't we all?
The good thing is that I can share it.

After all the years
I think this church is for me!
I'm glad I don't have to say its name often –
WOOLWICH COMMUNITY CHURCH ICHTHUS.
What a mouthful!
Add the address,
Even more of a mouthful!

22nd May 2002

"*Graham and Angela moved to a church in Spain. Woolwich Church left Ichthus in 2014/2015.*"

Chapter Two

In this section, I ask questions about my relationship with God, the Church and the way I am feeling now.

My experience of other churches was that I got so far and then felt that a wall was preventing me from feeling part of the church, and I tended to drop out. At Ichthus Church on Woolwich Common, I found that I enjoyed going, that people were more welcoming and I got further than before. Although at times I felt that wall was still there, I was more prepared to struggle against it than to run away.

John and I went there for a few years, then he left. I left a good few years after him.

I have questions I cannot find the answer to, especially regarding my disability.

I would like you to be aware that some of these poems go deep into my feelings and I hope they will not depress you too much. I hope that you can learn through them that there are ways that you can help people with disabilities, like myself. By giving me time, by getting to know me and giving me the chance to prove that I am just like everybody else.

I may never find the answers to some of my questions.

WAITING

"After my eye operation, a nurse had to put eye drops in my eyes a few times a day for a few weeks as John was at work. When the eye-drop times came down to evenings and mornings, we said goodbye to the nurses. **"**

Waiting, waiting, waiting
Is all I seem to be doing
Can't concentrate on anything
Can't do anything
Just sit there and wait!
Have to be on guard just in case I miss them
Waiting for John
Need not worry as he has the keys
Waiting for the professionals
Can be within half an hour

Waiting for Jo
Can be ten minutes either way
Waiting for Tracey
Within twenty minutes unless there is traffic
Waiting for Helen
Within five minutes unless there is traffic
Waiting for church members
Some are early – and I mean early
Some are late – what can I say?
But when waiting for the *nurses*!
THE WORST OUT OF THE LOT!

So while sitting waiting
Getting bored and wondering
My blindness and deafness make it difficult
My flashing light doesn't always help
So sitting there near the door
Looking through the little window
My mind seems to wander and sometimes goes into prayer.

1st October 2001

Me Now, Me Then

I am blind but have limited sight.
I am deaf but hear certain speech.
My speech is odd, caused by old habits.
My arms, hands, legs and feet cause me trouble,
As if they live in a world of their own.

Disabled from birth – became part of me.
Could read, watch TV, now listen.
Could hear with my eyes, noisy aid.
Can talk, need more care and time
With writing and phoning, change hands.
Could walk unaided,
Now need a wall, an arm or wheelchair.

Being turned upside down
Left me questioning,
Is God in control in any of this?
I know in my heart, Jesus is with me,
Jesus is carrying me through.

1st June 2001

Disappointed

Months and days are flying by,
Hours and minutes are ticking on,
My eye is seeing deeper grey.
The cataract is getting closer.
My time was up to have it checked.
When I heard the words, my heart sank with fear.
The thought of going through that again,
Eye drops, keeping head still, keeping eye open,
And capsules to swallow this time . . .
Glaucoma, glaucoma, oh dear.
If only I had known,
I would have gone back months ago.

Within forty-eight hours my faith is destroyed.
Not praying like I should,
Feel I'm letting people down.
At least I'm saying a prayer,
Gets repeated four times a day,
The Lord's Prayer, *Our Father . . .*

Two weeks have gone by,
And I am just feeling the same.
This shell I'm in – I must get out.
Telling people how I feel doesn't help,
All their nice words are meaningless at the time,
But, wow, later, in a few days' time,
Only God is the one who can help.

Trying to find my way out of my shell,
As I feel so low,
Should I go on blaming myself?
As God knows my heart,
I am trying to find my faith again.
How long will it take to find a way?
For God knows the answer,
As time goes by, so will I,
Thinking of the poem 'Footprints'
For those who know it
Will understand what I mean.

24th June 2001

ME AND GOD?

Listening to a friend's tape,
Sitting in my armchair,
Thinking about me and God,
I start talking to God.

Why me? Why not me?
Where am I going?
What is happening to me?
When is God going to intervene?
What am I living for?
How much longer can I go on like this?

I long to get back to how I was.
Healing – when will it come?
It is overdue.
Church or house group can't give me answers;
It is just the way I feel.

What does God want of me?
I need not worry.
God knows my heart.
Need to get back to prayer.
I need to learn to trust Him!

11th–24th October 2001

ANOTHER DAY

Oh dear, another day,
Just like any Monday, Wednesday or Friday.
John been and gone,
Done me shoes up,
Done me eye drops,
Got my breakfast out
And other bits 'n' bobs
And of course my tablet.

Just three hours to play with.
Know what I should do:
Listen to the Bible, but I can't.
Should worship but don't feel like it.
Slowly getting back into prayer.
Should I listen to the music? Maybe.
Should I go on the computer? Depends on my eye.
Should I go to sleep? Feel it is a waste
But these drugs are making me tired.

Ah, twelve noon, Jimmy Young,
The Archers and other topics.
Look forward to Joanne
As she'll cheer me up.
She's such a hard-working lady.
When she finishes, we say bye-bye.

Then I look forward to John again.
First, our supper or go on the computer,
Listen to *The Archers*,
My eye drops again,
A TV programme or listen to some music,
Then my tablet again, not only one but plus a half.
He reads to me, then helps me go to bed.
Won't go to sleep until John phones me.
Say my last prayer.
Off to sleep I go.
When I wake up,
Oh dear, another day again!

7th–13th August 2001

I Wonder

What is going on in me?
For the past few days
Haven't been feeling well
Tummy ache
Legs jerking
Eye getting worse
Not eating properly doesn't help
Not enough to say I'm ill
Got no energy in me
Is it the drugs I'm taking?
God seems so far away
Have a lot on my mind
The operation is one
The carer is next
Rod at the day centre
And of course my friends
The only thing I can do is pray
Even that seems hopeless at times
I wonder what God is thinking

I do wish I could walk without holding
I do wish I could see to read my Bible
Hearing it on tape is not the same
I wish for some visitors from the church
To study the Bible or to have a chat
Would make all the difference to me
I feel useless and left out
It's not the real me
Jesus lives in me and I in Him
Do I need to worry?
He knows my heart, thoughts and feelings
He will do what is best for me
He has shown me through the carer
Some people are around when I cry
But John is the one that hears the most
John's my closest friend among others

18th July–3rd August 2001

QUESTION

What on earth is going on inside me?
The operation tomorrow
My legs are just the same
No better, no worse
Might need two hearing aids
Whatever is going to happen next?
I am really getting fed up
How much longer can I go on?

House group didn't help
I felt down and worried
Couldn't concentrate on anything
Members were very kind to me
We were all anointed with oil
We started praying
Closed my eyes – all I could see was blackness
Where is God in what's happening?
Where is he leading me?
These questions are in my mind
They keep me thinking
The meeting came to an end
Was I glad or disappointed?
I leave this open, you decide

17th August 2001

Church

I look forward to church
When I get there I feel disappointment
Just a building
My blindness takes over
Can't see the individual
Unless they are close to me
I know my friends are around
Do they know this?
Do they think I am being rude
If I don't answer them?

I feel like a dummy sitting there
I feel like a dummy during worship
I can't join in the singing
Unless I know the words
Or the Spirit takes over
If neither, I used to go into prayer
Don't seem able to now
I'm wondering why

After the service
To the café for a hot chocolate
I begin to feel lost
Waiting for 'Hi, Julia'
If it comes
I cheer up
I feel better
I feel I belong

28th–31st October 2001

FEELING LOST

Went to church early
As John was on duty.
Music playing in the background
I began thinking
What am I doing here?
I feel Jesus is far away.
I can't get close to Him.
Something is in the way.
What – I don't understand.
Maybe I should leave.
That wouldn't be the answer.
Hearing, 'Oh, I believe in you, Lord'
Fills me with the Spirit – I join in.

In the service I am told
Jesus is for me and has plans for me.
What are they?
I want to open my heart to Jesus.
I want to get close to Him.
I can't.
Yet I am filled with the Holy Spirit.
Do I need to let myself go?
What do I need?
I cannot see the path ahead

I leave feeling odd.
Is it bitterness I feel?
John thinks I feel lost.
Maybe, maybe not.
I ask myself, 'Where do I go?'
What does HE want?

4th–8th November 2001

THE BRICK WALL

Oh dear, oh dear
Not again
A black cloud is over me
A brick wall in front of me
I can't break through
Stops me from reaching God
What do I do?
Leave the Church?
Stop praying?
Close my Bible?

No, no, I will fight against it.
Months ago
I went forward for prayer.
It didn't help.

Shared it with Graham, our pastor.
Knew that he could help.
Talked and prayed.
The black cloud has gone.

The brick wall I can see
Is my relationship with God,
How I see myself as a Christian.
I can't get right with God.
Should I give up?
Are past experiences in my way?
Am I becoming more disabled?
When fellow Christians help me
Is it real friendship or for show?

Can't keep running away!
I want to be back with Jesus.
Sharing my feelings with Graham,
Finding my path back to Jesus.

27th July 2002

Chapter Three

I don't think anyone can tell what is going to happen in the future. Only God knows that. But we can all have imagination, dreams and ideas of we would like to happen.

I have written a few poems about how I see God working in me in the future. There is one poem about times when I have been really high with God, and there is another poem about how I think God is going to lead me in the future.

What Am I Learning?

What am I learning?
What is God teaching me?
Is he training me for something?
I know what I am experiencing:
Mum's experiences of disability.
Mum didn't like depending on people,
I don't.
Mum didn't like waiting for people,
I don't.
Mum wanted to be independent,
So do I.
Mum had to use a wheelchair in the end,
Now I do.
Mum lost one leg, then the other,
I lost my sight in one eye.
Will I lose my other eye?
Mum lived alone with Social Services' help,
Now I do.
I see Dad in John,
Dad caring for his wife,
John caring for his friend.

I ask myself,
What is God doing?
Am I being tested?
Why, why, why?
Where is it leading me?
Not bringing me closer to Jesus.
It makes it harder for me.
I'm fed up with suffering.
It never seems to end.
What am I supposed to do?
Will I ever get better?
It seems to go on and on.
A better tomorrow?
Will it ever come?

4th August 2002

Blindness (2)

Ever since Monday
At the eye clinic
Told for sure
What is going to happen
Do I feel better?
Does it make it worse?

Plays on my mind
How can I cope?
As it grows worse
I keep thinking
People are around me
But if I keep on
Will they get fed up?

Deep in my heart
Do I trust God?
I wonder
My faith is up
My faith is down
God knows the outcome
Why can't I believe
I will not go blind?

If it goes wrong
What will I do?
Will I get more care?
Will I have to pay for it?
What will I do with my time?
People don't visit me now!
Will they if I'm blind?
Three or four will

How will I see the church?
How will I see God?
Will it draw me closer to Jesus?
Or will I walk away?

27th February 2002

I Never Thought

I never thought I would go blind in one eye,
Partially sighted in the other.
I never thought I would end up in a wheelchair,
Unable to walk without a hand.

What have I done to deserve this?

Looking back over the years,
Did I take my life for granted?
Should I have left Ladywell Centre years ago
When the WRVS didn't give me what I wanted?

I feel my life has been wasted.
Should I have taken more risks?
Would my life have been different?

Life is about taking risks.
Is Jesus in me or not?

Counselling and teaching courses,
A degree as well.
I am a better person all round.

What does the future hold?
If I had taken another path
Where would I be now?
Does it matter?
Asking these questions,
Is it *pointless*?
God planned my life
Long before I was born.
Everything works for the good of God?

27th June 2002

TREES

Springtime and autumn-time
Are the best times.
Springtime,
Buds grow different shades of green.
Summertime,
The birds nest in the trees,
Squirrels are playing.
Autumn-time,
Leaves are wet and slimy
Or dry and crumble into nothing.
Wintertime,
Snow on the trees
Reminds you of Christmas.

A tree is the world.
The branches are different nations.
The leaves are the groups that make up a nation.

The trunk is Jesus.
The branches are stages in my life as I grow up.
The leaves are my experiences in life.
I'm halfway up the tree.
When I reach the top I join Jesus.

1st January 2013

Jesus

How do I see Jesus?
What does Jesus mean to me?
What are my feelings for Him?
To be honest, I don't know.
I know He gave his life for me.
I know He loves and cares for me.
He is the same always.
He never changes.

I never get excited like some Christians do.
I know He is there, though I can't see Him.
People will let you down without meaning to.
Jesus will never let you down.

I know when Jesus is in me.
He gives me a warm feeling,
A feeling of contentment.
I know when he wants me to do something
He makes me go all hot.
I hate it.
He doesn't make you do what he asks.
He just asks again later.
It's better for me to do it there and then.

I can cry, scream and shout at Him.
I can't talk to Him as a friend.
I cannot understand why.
I can never be sure He is listening.
I am not always sure it is Him who helped me.
In my heart, I believe He is there,
Supporting me through my daily life.

22nd March 2004

GOING FORWARD

Looking back over my Christian life
I am slowly beginning to realise what is going on
During the last few months, my friend has hit the key
And I never realised it before

When I first became a Christian
I looked around the room and everything seemed different
Everything, even the chairs and table, looked more real and true
That is the only way I can describe it
I know it was something God had planned for me, but it soon went away
I felt lost, feeling that God was not there

Over the years I have had high moments
When I have been really close to God
They have usually come when I was praying or worshipping
Or listening to the Bible

I heard from someone you never get the same feeling twice
But God always touches you in different ways
This has encouraged me to constantly aim at
Getting back to a closer relationship with God again

So forward, onward I go
Waiting for the Lord to touch me again

Chapter Four

It was during 2012 that I started writing poetry again, and here are my latest poems. They are not all about real things as in previous poems. They are more about everyday life and about my feelings.

I try to treat all my PAs the same. There are days when I'm in a mood and my ways change from one PA to the next. Sometimes, I can be jolly with one and just want to be quiet or left alone with the other, not to keep being asked what I want to do.

I must say Jo, Tim and Wayne are very good PAs and look after me really well. I couldn't ask for anyone better.

SuperNova

SuperNova, *SuperNova*,
What a program it was and still is.
I used to use it a lot at one stage.
It was very good as it read text out to me.
Whatever I typed, it could read or magnify it.
It had one bad habit of repeating itself;
This would drive everybody mad in my place.
I upgraded the program twice.

Computer kept crashing, then packed up.
John and I bought a replacement.
SuperNova wouldn't work.
Two years went by before I did anything.
Bought *SuperNova* 2012 version.
We couldn't start it, let alone use it.
UCanDoIT, Mike came along,
Introduced me to *Guide* program.
What a change it made to my life!
Now I can use the computer again!
Fantastic, fantastic.

5th October 2012

JUMBULANCE

JUMBULANCE on a JOURNEY,

J = Joining in and joking about,
U = Understanding each other,
M = Meeting new people,
B = St Bernadette, bringing old friends together,
U = Undergoing changes,
L = Lourdes and learning,
A = Accessibilities,
N = Nurses,
C = Caring for each other,
E = Enjoying ourselves, ending holiday, exhausted by some!
      23rd June 2013

JUMBULANCE

Jumbulances are special coaches,
Designed for disabled or sick people,
Six beds on one side,
Twenty seats on the other side,
At the back a kitchen and a toilet.
In blue and white, a welcome sight,
Carrying disabled pilgrims,
Helpers, nurses, a doctor and a chaplain,
On their way to Lourdes,
Where St Bernadette grew up,
Where she met the Virgin Mary.
We visit the Sanctuary and the Grotto,
We go to Mass in the Basilicas,
We go to an open-air Mass.

There is also a lovely trip up the mountain,
Round and round we go until we reach the top.
The mountain is higher than the road, pointed to the sky.
Watching the water going down is so peaceful.
Sometimes you can see some snow on top.
A big party night, everyone takes part in it,
With a three-course meal, then the party starts.
Those who dress up, some can sing or act,
The fun and laughter that comes with it.
That is our latest night of the week.
The time we get back to the hotel and get to bed
Could be after midnight in some cases.
We do get well looked after by the helpers.
The helpers do all the packing, making sure you get everything including
    your journey bag.
Some are sad as the holiday is coming to an end.
If you go again, like I have, you can meet old friends,
Can make long or short term friends and can keep in touch.
We come home all happy and jolly,
The helpers go home tired and exhausted,
But it's been worth every minute of the trip.

28th June 2013

INSIDE

Not everybody will know this,
Or understand what I feel,
When it comes to handling me.
Sometimes it is my fault,
Because of the way I hold myself,
Other times it is the carer's fault,
Or it can be the fault of both of us,
When I say it is hurting me.
This is where I break down.
We argue against each other,
Trying to reason why, this or that,
Which is what I don't need.
Is that person inside my body,
To tell me when I'm being hurt?
Even though one doesn't mean to,
It is too late to do or to say anything.
Some say I'm putting it on;
How can I when I'm feeling pain?
God, where are you in all this?
I can't take much more of this!
You allow me to go through it,
Help me to learn to stay calm,
As Jesus is going through this with me!

30th April 2013

If Only I Could ...

If only I could stand, walk a step or two;
  My wheelchair is my legs.
If only I could go out on my own;
  I have to be taken by someone.
If only I could use my hands better;
  My carers act as my hands.
If only I could feed myself;
  My PAs put food into my mouth.
If only I could see to read a book;
  The DAISY player reads it out to me.
If only I could hold a pen to write;
  Friends do the writing for me,
  Or hold a pen in my hand to write.
If only I could take myself to the loo;
  My helpers have to take me.
If only I could dress myself;
  Whoever is on duty will dress me.
If only I could undress myself;
  My friend has to undress me.
If only I could put myself to bed;
  My friend puts me to bed.
If only I could turn over in bed,
  Instead of staying in one spot.
How I would love to turn back the clock,
  To when I could do all these things myself!
1st May 2013

If I Could ...

I wish I could turn the clock back
To the years of the seventies and eighties,
And, of course, the early nineties.
Living at home, then Bargery Road,
They were my happy times.
When I could do almost anything,
Go anywhere in London on my own,
But needed a bit of help here and there.
Move away from my friends, which is for the best.
Be nearer to John as he is my friend and carer.
If I'd stayed in Lewisham, would I have got a bungalow?
Only God knows the answer to that question.
Here I am now in the twenty-first century;
My life has been turned upside down.
Now I'm completely dependent on people.

7th May 2013

Where Would I Be ...

Where would I be if I be if I didn't have good parents?
　Probably in a home.
Where would I be without special schooling?
　Probably sent to a boarding school.
Where would I be if I didn't go to a day centre?
　Probably be at home, bored.
Where would I be if I didn't go to college?
　Wouldn't have received my qualifications.
Where would I be if I hadn't become a Christian?
　Jesus wouldn't be in my life.
Where would I be if I didn't have my friends?
　I would be lonely.
Where would I be without technology?
　Technology wasn't around when I was young.
Where would I be if I didn't have *Guide* software?
　Absolutely lost.
Where would I be without Jo, Helen and John?
　They play a big part in my life!

8th May 2013

I Don't Know Where I Stand

I don't know how I feel at the moment.
I know it's not what I should feel.
Has to do with my relationship with God.
I wish I could go back to 1980 or 2000,
When I felt Jesus' touch.
Now I feel so far away from Him.
Is it what I have done in my life? No!
Depends on how much time I spend with Jesus.
Worship is important to God.
I can only sing old worship songs.
I wonder if God gets fed up with this?
As I can't see to read the words.
Listening to the words doesn't help either;
The music can overtake the wording.
I find it hard to pray from time to time,
Feel like I'm not getting anywhere.
Church is another problem for me;
Even though I know I should go
There are too many problems.
Maybe I haven't found the right one yet.
Jesus, will I ever find a church for me?

10th May 2013

Helen

I met Helen over twelve years ago,
Through my care manager at that time.
Her children were young then;
Now they are grown up in universities.
Her job is a communicator guide.
Helen first came to me on Friday mornings.
We got on well together the first week we met.
Was easier to collect her son from a nursery.
We had a lot of fun and we still do!
Didn't know very much about computers,
But was a very good typist and could use the phone!
When the computer played up,
It was our fault in pressing the wrong key!
When John came over to use the computer, he would say,
'You've been at it again!'
I would keep my mouth shut and leave it to him.
It was easier to fix on some days than others.
Then she switched to Monday afternoons.
I didn't know whether she was coming or not.
I got disappointed when she would phone to say she couldn't come on
    that day; I still do.
I would say, 'Oh no, I've got to wait until next week.'
Helen helped me to meet my sister.
Her teaching job would make Helen late!
The staff were putting more work into her hands.
Now my friend John is at my place,
We all get on and have a laugh together.
Sometimes I have to break the conversation.
Helen had less time to do the jobs I had for her but we always managed to
    get them done!
Then she got a new job out of the blue.
I was very pleased for her.
I was afraid that I might lose Helen!
I just couldn't start again with a new person.

I wasn't going to let her leave me that easy.
I'm glad to see Helen is still working for me.
She is a brilliant worker and a good friend!
I always look forward to seeing Helen as she cheers me up.
I know Helen does cheer up John too!
   15th May 2013

"In 2014, after fifteen years of working as a communicator guide, Helen had to get a full-time job. Her daughter, Louise, and her son, Thomas, were at university. Helen needed more pay. Helen visited me once a month for a drink and a chat."

Carers

I know I need help these days,
In order to get through the day.
I have four good carers.
What would I do without them?
I know I would be stuck.
Sometimes one or two will get me angry,
Then I wish that PA would go away;
I just want to be left alone to do my own thing.
They all have their own way of doing things.
Some are better than the others.
It is hard to treat them all the same,
But I try to do my best for each one.
I can get on with one more than the others.
Depends on how I feel on the day.
One of my PAs is brilliant,
Who would do almost anything.
One of them is my close friend,
Who is always there for me,
During the evening when the others are off,
In the early hours when emergencies can arise.
Doesn't get paid for all the hours he gives me.
I often wonder what my future would be
If anything happened to my close friend.
He will be very hard to replace!

18th May 2013

LIVING

What is life?
Life is from when you are born until you die.
Life is what you make of it.
God gives you a choice,
To follow Him or to go your own way;
You can choose your path.
I am tired and fed up with life,
Even though I have a good one.
I have done and achieved a lot.
Technology has made my life a lot easier.
I am getting tired of living.
My disability has been part of me since birth.
In recent years I became more disabled.
This made me question God – *Why?*
What have I done wrong?
I am fed up depending on people.
Don't really know what I am hoping for.
God has allowed me to experience it.
Can God use me like this?
I know Jesus can heal even today,
I have God's word and promise on this.
I keep asking and praying about it,
But no answer comes.
Am I not hearing the Holy Spirit?
When people say God is in control I get angry.
If they say God decides when, I get angry,
So what do I do now?
I am tired of waiting!

24th May 2013

FRIENDS

It's good how we make friends during our lifetime,
Some we keep in touch with for years.
Friends will come and go.
Rosemary was my first school friend,
We went to a club and swimming together,
During my secondary school she was a great help when we went out
    together.
Somehow we lost contact and never met again.
Elaine and Janet were my next friends,
Went swimming on Wednesday evenings.
Hear about Elaine and Janet from time to time.
Lorraine and I used to go to Girl Guides,
We were named the Terrible Twins,
We would always fall into trouble and couldn't be broken apart when we
    were together!
We are still in touch today.
At Trinity Centre were Derek, Charlie, Mick and Alan, who I was very
    close to, now have passed away.
Melita was very good to me with writing and helping me with personal
    things,
We still keep in touch as she has moved away.
Pat helped me with my Christian faith,
Now she visits me once a month for coffee and a chat.
From here Hilda played a part by supporting me in so many ways.
At Ladywell Centre there were quite a few staff I made friends with –
    Maurice, Carole, Ester and Sid, Kieran, Alan, Dawn and lastly John who
    is now my close friend and my carer.
In the WRVS shop there – the two Renées; Victor, who asked me to take
    the shop over; Mary, who used to buy my can of Coke for me. Sylvia
    became a great friend and when we both left she would visit me once a
    month for a very long chat and a mug of tea.
These friends are no longer with me.
During my college years I had made friends but didn't keep in touch for
    very long.

Been to different churches, known lots of members but often wonder how
    they are.
Now I meet friends like Frank, Barbara, Hilda, Lorraine and Margaret
    when we fix a date.
I often think about the ones I don't hear from,
Wondering what they are doing.
Everybody needs a friend.
A friend can be your companion.

26th May 2013

16/12/2012

Jo

I first met Jo in 2001,
She was sent by GAD.
Jo was my first personal assistant.
I thought she was a little madam.
She looked bossy to me,
As she sat there silently.
She did two hours Monday to Friday.
She did housework and my laundry.
We went to Woolwich to shop.
I liked her more and more.
She had a car and we went out on short journeys
To a pub or a park,
To hospital or the dentist.
Jo is a brilliant worker,
Good with her hands, whatever it might be!
Jo took me to the dentist and hospitals.
I became more disabled; she worked more hours.
Jo could put her hands to anything.
Bombshell, Jo was going to Spain,
To join her boyfriend.
She stayed while I had a serious eye operation.
My care manager kept on at me to replace Jo.
I hoped Jo would come back.
Eventually I tried to replace her, no one could.
I kept hoping that she would come back.
It was difficult to keep in touch.
I gave up hope she would come back.
Four years later she phoned me,
She was home, could she pop round?
Jo and her boyfriend were home looking for work.
They were redundant, Spain was in trouble.
I offered her job back; yes, she said.
I was so happy.
Four hours, four days a week, fantastic!

Jo had a boy and we love hearing about him.
She has good support from family and partner.
Jo takes me to see shows,
She goes on holiday with me.
Jo is always helpful and flexible.
We miss her when she's not here.
Jo has a heart of gold.

28th May 2013

"GAD (Greenwich Association of Disabled People) is no longer there."

16/12/2012

I Don't Mean To

I don't mean to, but I do.
I tend to pick on John.
We wind each other up.
Most of the time he wins.
I get uptight and angry with him.
I get angry with him over silly little things.
I don't mean to, but that's the way I am.

I don't mean to, but I do.
I tend to hit John with my feet,
By accident; I can't see where my feet go,
But they always seem to get him.
My wheelchair also gets told off,
As John does walk into it.
I don't mean to.
It is beyond my control.

I try to make things easier or quicker
When dressing or undressing me,
To save time and energy just like my mum.
John just doesn't want to know.
He is happy doing things his own way.
Then we start shouting at each other for a bit.
I don't mean to, but I care.

I get frustrated when I can't hear what he said,
But then he doesn't always hear me.
John will say I didn't say it when I did.
I don't mean to, but this will make me mad.
I know how much I rely on him.
He is the closest one to me.
We spend a lot of time together;
This causes us to have so many ups and downs.
People say we are like a married couple.
We both say we are glad we are not.
We do have a strong friendship.
It is the way I am, I go round in circles.
I don't mean to, but I do.

31st May 2013

FREEDOM

"I wrote this poem in the 1970s when I was at Trinity Day Centre. I can remember tearing it up because I didn't like the way I ended the poem."

Maybe I was shy in those days!
It was a lovely sunny afternoon.
I was getting a bit fed up sitting around here,
Feeling hot and seeing how cool it looks outside.
I decided to take a walk up the park,
Which was only ten minutes away from Trinity.
When I arrived at the park,
The path was quite a hill pointing to the sky.
As I was walking up it,
The sun was shining down on my back,
Making me feel really hot and sticky.
When I reached the top it was spaceless,
Grass on either side, nowhere to sit,
All I could see around me
Different shapes and sizes of chimney pots.
I was the only person here.
What a lovely feeling it gave me being up here.
I stayed there for fifteen minutes staring into space.
I turned round to make my way back to Trinity,
Running down the hill as if to fall into a man's arms,
But when I reached the bottom
There was nobody there, only me.

10th June 2013

What Is Going to Happen ...

I often wonder about my future.
My disability has worsened over the last few years,
I am relying on more and more care,
So what is going to happen when I get old?
Especially when John can no longer care for me
Or when John is no longer with me;
I know that day will come.
Will I be ready for it?
Will I be able to cope?
I do think about this from time to time.
I know that John does think about it too,
Every now and again just like I do.
Will Jo, Helen and other friends be here,
Or will they move on?
Nobody knows, only God.
Friends say I shouldn't worry, but I do.
Some say I might be healed,
Then my worry has been for nothing.
I would love to be healed any time now.
Only God knows the answer to that question.
John and I both know what the real worry is:
Who is going to take his place as a carer with the hours, time and
    friendship he gives me?
And, just as importantly, who will do my finances?
We know who we would like that person to be.
Once again, only God knows the answer to that question.

11th June 2013

What's Wrong

It is one of those days.
I woke up with a stiff neck,
But felt OK – John helped as usual.
Went to listen to some music,
Then listened to the Bible.
Said a prayer for Jo as she isn't well.
Sitting in my wheelchair saying,
How lucky I am to have things near me:
Two players – one for the Bible,
The other one for talking books,
A CD player to play music to suit my mood,
Or listen to the radio, if I wanted to,
On top of this I could even watch a DVD.
At midday John was ready to collect my prescription,
He came back before going down the road.
I decided to do something on the computer.
Sitting at the computer not knowing what to do,
My mind wasn't here or there,
As the mood I was in had changed.
I often wonder why I get these moods.
Does it have anything to do with God?
Is it to do with my prayer life?
Or not spending time with Him?
Typing this poem has cheered me up,
And now it's nearly time for John to have his nap!
And for Wayne to come to cook our dinner.
In two hours Wayne will be gone,
Monday is nearly over, tomorrow is another day,
So we start all over again.

17th June 2013

THUNDER

A good few years ago,
Before I ended up in a wheelchair,
On one Wednesday evening,
I would be at John's flat on the fourth floor,
Facing the back of Woolwich Common.
I knew we were going to get a storm,
The weather was hot and sticking.
Standing outside on his balcony,
As I could see for miles across the sky,
I could hear roaring thunder in the distance,
The flashing lightning coming across the sky,
Some bolts straight and others weaving bright light with blue edges.
Thunder clashing louder and louder by the minute,
The rain was pouring from the sky,
My head was getting wet from the balcony above.
I put both my hands out to get them wet,
To wet my face to feel how cool the rain was.
The lightning was slowly disappearing,
The thunder roared louder over Woolwich Common,
Then it went quieter and quieter till I could hear it no more.
Standing there on the balcony as if nothing had happened.
What a beautiful sight it was.

21st June 2013

Ladywell Day Centre

I used to love going to the old Ladywell.
As I walk through the main entrance,
Going past the old building,
Bending down here and there,
I can see underneath the building,
Nothing but cobwebs, spiders and dust,
A, B, C block part of the old workhouse.
I believe there were two floors with an old-fashioned lift.
During the early seventies, I could see some beds when it used to be a
    ward at one time.
There were also some pictures of the workhouse in action.
Once inside the C block with other members,
All the fun I could get up to lay ahead of me.
Could it be with Charlie, Mick or Paul?
There was always somewhere to hide.
Would I be with some of my other friends to get out of physio?
It was true on some Tuesdays.
I did try to get out of it.
It is lovely walking over the footbridge in the summer,
There is a stream going through,
I would stay there for quite a while watching the water flow through.

In the winter I would hurry across the footbridge to keep warm.
In the seventies they knocked down the A, B and C blocks and built a new
    Ladywell Day Centre.
I could still get up to fun but not like I could in the old workhouse
    building.

29th June 2013

"*Before 1977, Ladywell Day Centre was a workhouse. For the
last thirty-eight years, it has catered for physically disabled
people. Now, in October 2015, it is going to be for people with
learning difficulties and dementia.*"

Dentist (1)

" This poem and the next two were written when I used to go to the dentist at Grove Park Hospital. It was knocked down during the late eighties to build houses and flats. The dentist was moved to Jenner Health Centre. "

The dentist is not my favourite date
But it's my fate and I feel faint
Past experiences I remember
I wish it was next December
The staff, though, are very nice
The injection put me out in a trice
That afternoon I came too
Extractions, fillings, crown
What a do
For seven days I paid the price
A sore mouth left me silent like mice
Would I have to live on rice?
But God knew best
Tamsin met the test
Kind, gentle and caring
Like the staff, she's the best
So this is to thank them all
They gave me confidence to dare all

2nd July 1991

Dentist (2)

I have been going to Kidbrooke Dentist
For nearly twelve years.
It was easy for me to get to.
Will never go without Jo, Tim or John taking me.
I still don't like going to the dentist.
I enjoyed meeting the staff I met over the years,
Caroline, Carol, Ruth, Nicky and many others.
I liked the bubblegum cream favour to numb my tooth before doing
     anything,
Having fillings, temporary crowns or teeth out without an anaesthetic.

After all these years I never thought or dreamt of allowing the dentist to
     take my teeth out
Without a general anaesthetic.
The injections were a bit painful.
I have really got my trust in that dentist.
I wonder what my mum is thinking in Heaven,
After all the trouble she went through to get me to go to the dentist when
     I was young.
I would like to think that Mums work has been paid off.

Now they have moved to a new building in Deptford.
Jo finds it hard to park her car near the place.
I have been transferred to another dentist which is even nearer than
     Kidbrooke,
And now I have got to start all over again,
Getting to know the new staff,
Wondering what they are going to be like,
But I still don't like going to the dentist.

8th July 2013

Dentist (3)

I visited my new dentist yesterday.
It is much easier to get to,
Plumstead instead of Kidbrooke.
The building has two disabled parking spaces,
An automatic door to let Jo and me in.
Waiting area is big and bright,
Didn't feel like I was closed in,
With long glass windows which made it friendly.
Also has a disabled toilet there.
Was feeling nervous but Jo kept me calm.
I was pleased to see Nicky working there today;
This also made me feel a lot better.
Once in the dentist's room plenty of space,
A dentist's armchair instead of a recliner.
Getting in the armchair is so much easier.
Mike, the dentist, sounds friendly.
I felt a bit tense once in the dentist's chair.
Mike started looking at my teeth.
He didn't hurt me one bit, not even my lips,
Not like the one at Kidbrooke did.
Mike's got the time to *listen* to me.
I think I'm going to enjoy coming here.

Mike has certainly won my *trust*;

The *real test* will come when I have got to have something done.

This will test his *patience* and *skill*,

Which is so important to me.

Oh dear, not another Mike.

I have a list of people with the same names,

John, Pat and now Mike!

Jo kept looking at Mike.

When Jo and I came out of the dentist she said, 'He is a spitting image of Tom's dad.'

'It's funny how you can sometimes see a person that reminds you of someone very close to you,' I said.

Jo answered, 'I know it wasn't him, but it just made me go blank for a few seconds.'

I then added, 'Well, you know what they say, everyone's got a double.'

12th July 2013

I Don't Really Like It

Set in my own way of having things done for me,
So when my PAs do a tiny thing differently,
I really don't like it,
As it can make me feel a bit frightened,
Unless that person tells me beforehand
How they are going to do something.
I like it done in a certain way if possible.
If my needs cannot be met on these grounds,
I tend to get cross or upset.

ALL I WANTED JOHN TO DO

I had to get John up to take me to the loo.
That went fine and no problem.
As it was 6.30 in the morning,
He put me back to bed for Tim to get me up at 9am.
What a palaver it was trying to get me comfortable.
Every few minutes I kept calling John back,
To pull my pillow this way and that way,
Putting my legs and bum in the right place,
Hoping that I would get comfortable.
This goes on for over half an hour.
I'm beginning to wonder whether it is worth it,
Going back to bed to listen to the radio in comfort.
I would rather be in bed all tucked up like a baby
Than being in my wheelchair.
Thank God I will be up in an hour and a half.
I can't stand all this palaver;
I'm sure John feels the same.
I know there is a quick and simple solution,
But we don't very often do it.
Is it because I don't tell John?
All he has to do is to get me up,
Pull down the bottom pillow a bit,
Then put me back to bed again!
This would save all the palaver of John coming to my bed every few
    minutes trying to get me comfortable!

3rd July 2013

"*After many months we manage to solve this problem by giving
me one pillow instead of two!*

*In July 2014, I went to Tenerife with Edna and Jo. Jo was
five months pregnant and was concerned about bending over
when putting me to bed. We took my slip mat, so quick
and easy to use. We just had to show John and he
has been using it ever since!*"

Sunday Afternoon

When the sun shines outside my bungalow,
It is lovely to go out and sunbathe
Even though I can only do my face, arms and sometimes my legs.
Sitting out there I don't feel I am in London,
As I live on the edge of an estate,
We have a driveway to park cars,
Can be hidden from the edge of the pavement,
Behind my flowerbed.
Most of the time it can be very quiet.
I just put my head back with my eyes closed,
Letting the sun burn down on me.
My mind begins to wander over all sorts of things,
Praying, God, Jesus and the Church.
John comes out every now and again to check if I'm OK and to see if I
    want anything.
Most of the time I will say, 'Ooh, yes, please, may I have a drink?'
Sometimes it will be a drink and a chocolate.
After this, I go back to my thinking world,
John, PAs, Frank, and some other friends.
I wish John would come out and join me,
He can't stand the hot weather like I can.
When I have enough of being in the sun,
I call John out to take me inside,
Until the next hot Sunday afternoon!

17th July 2013

ONE EVENING

On one evening, after a boiling hot day,
Sitting outside my bungalow near the front door,
It was so peaceful when the noisy kids had disappeared.
I started to wander off as usual, thinking.
I found myself asking God these questions:
'What do you want from me?
What do you want me to do?
What am I learning through this?
Why am I like this?'
In a wheelchair, partially sighted and deaf,
I know I do more than some people do.
I am so glad for that.
I can't just sit still and not do anything.
I feel so much like Job in the Bible.
The wind is slowly increasing across my face,
Which is bringing me back to earth.
I thank God for listening to me.
The wind is getting stronger and cooler.
As John comes out to take me back indoors,
I say, 'Thank you, Lord, for making me as I am!'

27th July 2013

RAIN

I have a pavement path outside my bungalow,
Which is under cover so that I don't get wet when getting in and out of a
  car.
When the light rain is coming down,
I don't know anything about it unless I'm told.
In the summer when we get a downpour or a cloudburst of rain, I love to
  be outside to listen to the sound it makes.
I love it when my PAs and John push me out into the rain for a few
  seconds to get the feel and the wetness.
I love it when I hear a car whoosh through a big puddle and especially
  when I'm in the car.
I love it when the rain is falling against the car roof and windows.
There is only one thing I really do miss;
I don't even know how much I could see of it,
But maybe I could see the movement it makes?
When the raindrops fall into puddles large or small,
From the centre outward,
It forms a shape of many rings.
They always remind me of a book called
The Lord of the Rings.

5th August 2013

ONE THING I WISH ...

There is only one thing I wish for,
And that is to be able to sing.
I know I can when I'm alone,
Or at church or in a group,
Or playing my CD extra loud,
So I can't hear what I sound like,
Especially when I don't know all the words.
I am shy and conscious of my voice.

I have heard someone say
That everybody can sing.
I believe you are born a singer,
Or train at a young age.
There are different types of voices,
Some I like more than others.
Does it depend on what you enjoy?
Or what mood we are in?

I have been told by my speech therapist,
If I practised singing,
It would do my breathing good
And improve my speech.
My friend Robert told me that too.
Some can talk better by singing,
Because it can slow you down,
As you sing the words clearer,
As you have to think more
When to take a breath,
Not like saying words naturally.
People say I talk better when I use
My robot voice!

30th December 2013

HOIST (1)

"I am so scared that I might have to use a hoist that hangs from the ceiling. I hope that day will never come, but I know it could in the future. I hate the whole idea. I started going to the gym, hoping in time my legs will get stronger and maybe I will be able to stand!"

I get angry and upset
If anyone mentions using a hoist.
It makes me feel I'm getting worse.
I feel it will be another step back,
I will lose the human contact.
Yes, I know I'm not thinking about my PAs,
The harm they could do to their backs
By lifting and holding me up.
A hoist is like a robot.
It depends on what one I use.
I have a standing-up one already.
By the time you strap me up and lift,
It could be too late for the toilet.
The thought and feeling I get as it comes towards me
Isn't a pleasant one.
I know that day will come.
I'm dreading it.
Tim, my PA, brought it up today,
He has pains in his back.
I went quiet and while I was having my shower
I told God about it, and John later.
John gave me his assurance,
And I like to believe Jo and Wayne will too,
Use a *hoist* when I really need to!

26th January 2014

Being Taken to the Loo

Never thought I would need help to go to the loo.
I never dreamt of needing someone to take me.
How embarrassing when I had to let someone help me,
Having to rely on somebody to put me on the loo.

I had thought about this for ages,
But tonight it was different,
As I had been more than usual.
It doesn't bother my PAs as I have four of them.
I have grown more conscious over the last few years,
Two PAs will leave me to it and wait until I call out, 'John,' or 'Jo.'
The other two can hear me or keep asking me if I am OK.
When I desperately want to go,
Some PAs will make me wait until they have finished their job.
At this moment how I wish I could just get up and go.
It makes it even harder when using the hoist.

Tonight, when I asked Wayne to put me on the loo,
A few minutes before his time was up,
It was so lovely to go in peace without anyone around.
John is asleep on my bed,
So I can relax a bit before I wake John,
To tell him I'm on the loo and ready to come off.

When Helen or Mike are working with me and I have to go,
They will either carry on working on the computer
Or get up and move around until I return.

It is true what people say,
You do get used to it.
I feel I like being helped by some more than others,
But it's not the same
As when you go on your own.

18th February 2014

Most People Have Someone

I have thought about this some time ago.
Yesterday I was thinking about it again.
Most people have someone to turn to.
How funny the way it works out.
Looking back over the years at the people I know,
How true it can be.
Apart from family members,
Husband and wife, partners,
Some get remarried,
And even today most of my friends
Have partners or close friends,
Most have sisters or brothers,
Some just have carers,
I have John, whom I have known for years.
It's the build-up of friendship,
Then it turns into *love* and *trust*!
I didn't know or plan for John to take care of me,
But he promised my mum that he would take care of me,
As Mum was worried what would happen when she passed away.
That was over thirty years ago!
Now in 2014 John has certainly kept his word.
I often wonder if God helps you to find someone.

2nd March 2014

THE THREE JOHNS

I know so many Johns,
I believe nine in all,
Some I don't hear from and some I do.
I have moved from Lewisham to Woolwich.
Some I met on holidays, apart from one
Whom I met at Ladywell in 1984,
Who I rely on so much now.
The second John I met on holiday in 2003
With Through the Roof to Cyprus.
He is understanding and can see both sides to a situation.
We have been to five different places over the years,
With his partner Georgie.
We phone each other and I see them whenever we can,
As they live in Bournemouth.
The other John I met through Jumbulance from 2009,
When I went to Lourdes.
He is just like the second John, but more joking,
He does like music and singing,
He lives in Northampton.
As the Jumbulance does more or less the same yearly,
He is such a busy man in my mind,
But I do see him and his friend Ann when they come to London.
I tend to see these two Johns as a father-type figure

30th March 2014

GUIDE VERSION 6 TO 8

I have been using *Guide*
For about a year now.
It has changed my life completely.
It has enabled me to use a computer again,
With my limited sight of 10%.
Guide is very good for emails, letters and voice memos.
You can do other things with *Guide*.
One good thing, I don't have to memorise anything,
Not like *SuperNova*,
But it does have a few bad points,
As when filling in forms and using the Internet,
What a palaver it can be.
I would be lost without it,
As there is so much you can do on *Guide*.

When I heard from Mike that
Dolphin had brought out Version 8,
Mike said they had improved it a lot,
Especially the Internet.
I would email Dale with most of my problems,
Or Mike if I could wait as he is a busy man.
Dale told me to play the demo of Version 8.
I thought, *Wow, how exciting.*
Jo and I went through it together.
It was dear but would be worth it.
After I ordered and paid for it, it came in three days.
I just couldn't wait to get it loaded,
But when I finally did,
It was well worth it.
Using the Internet is so much better.
What a great improvement Version 8 is.
Versions 9 and 10 will be out soon.
Wow, I can't wait.

14th April 2014

Occupational Therapist (1)

The thought of an occupational therapist
Paying me a home visit to find out what aid I need.
John, Tim, Jo and I all know what it's to do with:
The standing-up hoist which I have.

I've been dreading this meeting for weeks on end,
Panicking, frightened, scared, worrying and wondering
What this occupational therapist will say,
Whether she will be on my side or the PAs' side, or both.

I knew Tim would be here but not John;
John will be having his dialysis.
I wanted Jo with me but not Wayne.
I won my wish and on the day I kept calm.

When Neil came I felt nervous but was in control,
Made sure that I let him know about my feelings regarding the hoist.
While Neil was talking and checking that he heard me
Jo and Neil went off to look at the hoist.
I'm sure Jo explained to Neil in more detail about my legs.

Tim, Jo and I demonstrated how we cope with the hoist.
Neil could understand the problems we are facing.
Neil told me that there are other hoists I can try out
Until we find the right one for me, which will take time.
As he is aware that we may or may not find one,
We will just have to wait and see; I know he will do his best.

It could be so easy for me to give up and hold my hands up,
To let the hoist do all the work,
Then I will get weaker.
While I'm using my legs they should get stronger.
I know it is hard for my PAs as accidents can happen,
But who suffers the most? I do.

I am pleased with the way the first meeting went.
I'm sure Neil and I will get on together.
I'm sure there are some things Neil will not understand,
Because he is not me,
But I will certainly put my trust in him.

23rd May 2014

KIERAN

Kieran came during the eighties
To work at Ladywell Day Centre.
He was a proper gentleman and still is.
Didn't take much interest in him at first,
Then we started talking here and there.
Kieran and I went out from time to time,
For a drink or to the cinema.
Happy being his friend.
2014, we are still in touch by email.
We do always try to meet up whenever I visit Ireland.
I often wonder how his family is getting on.

Me, living in Bargery Road,
Which I was at that time during the eighties;
Kieran sometimes cooked us a meal
When he used to live nearby.
All of a sudden he asked me to look after his goldfish,
While he went home to Cork for the weekend.
I made sure he collected it on Monday.
I was worried about caring for it.
Changing the water was fun.
Slowly the fish stayed with me longer and longer.
In the end the fish became mine for good.

On a day outing with the centre,
I asked the staff if Kieran could be Mum's helper.
I won my wish, and the fun we had that day.
Even Mum was amazed how he managed to get her into a tiny little craft
    shop.

Kieran went home to Ireland for good.
I visited him twice on my own,
Will always remember when he drove me round Kerry.
Then he married, built a home and had a family.
John, Edna and I have met his wife, Paula, and children.
We will never forget his friend and the meal at the Titanic restaurant – it
    was out of this world,
Everything was absolutely superb.

Last year, Jo, Edna and I visited Ireland.
Kieran and his son, David, travelled for miles to see me.
Kieran and I will be friends for life.

29th June 2014

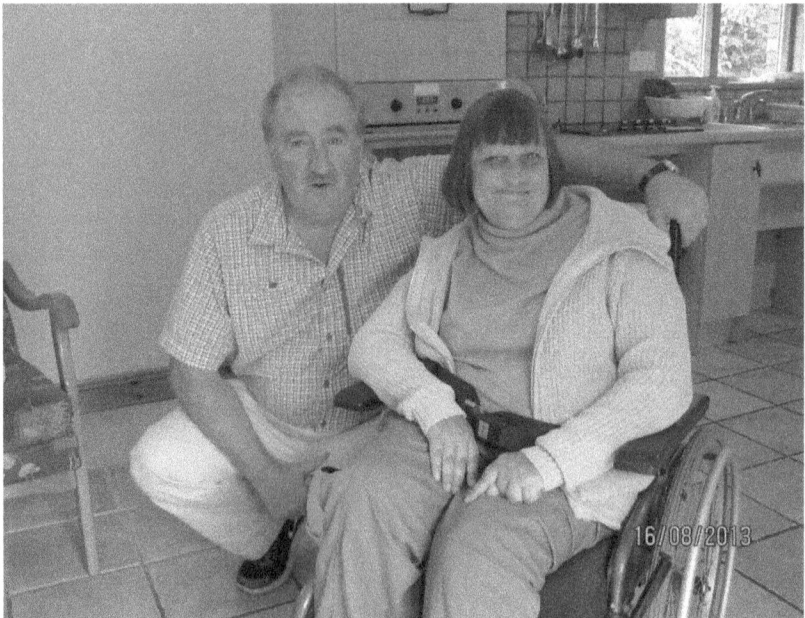

Books

As far back as I can remember,
I have always loved books.
First, Mum taught me to read
Using *Janet and John* books,
Then on to *Look and Learn* mag.
I used to love the yearly annuals,
Especially *The Girl Guides* and *Look and Learn*.

As I grew older and began to buy books,
I loved the smell, feel and the touch of the pages.
I would spend hours in the bookshops,
Just looking and skipping through them,
Putting the book back where I got it from.

Next was the library – full of books everywhere,
Once inside, books on any subject.
Used to love using the index cards to find the shelf;
I felt important, as if I worked there.
Nowadays, everything is computerised,
Just sit at the keyboard, type in the author etc.,
Within a few seconds all sorts of information.
I could stay there for hours looking up books,
Forgetting myself, time just rushing by, late for my next appointment,
Whether for the day centre, college, dentist or home.
There is so much more we can get in a library today.

Now I am blind, I can't read books today,
Rely on talking books which I play on my DAISY player.
Don't like all books from the Home Library Service,
As there can be something wrong with some;
Frustrating only to listen to a bit,
Especially when it's read to you by someone famous,
Then have to return it,
Not knowing how the book finishes,
Especially when I remember the introduction.
The RNIB or the Calibre libraries are the best,
Just go onto their websites and click on as many books as I want,
Calibre and RNIB library will send me four from each,
After listening to three or five I return them, then my next titles are sent.
Some books can have anything up to sixteen hours on one CD,
So I can never run out of a talking book.

30th August 2014

An Accident

Turning to one side to stop and watch,
Amazed at what I could see,
Never seen anything like it, so many vehicles,
It must be during the rush hour.
Four lines of steady driving and an outer line,
All sorts of cars, different shapes, sizes and colours,
Lorries, different lengths, heights, widths and depths,
Coaches with their company name and colours,
Then within a split second I saw a line of cars
Driving into a lorry which stopped out of the blue.
There were about nine cars in the pile-up.
Next I could hear police cars, fire engines, ambulances approaching
    everywhere,
Loads of them.
If I was asked to give details, I couldn't,
It happened so quick.
The traffic police took care of the traffic,
Closing and directing drivers from both ends,
At the same time firemen were working on the cars,
Broken glass and petrol all over the place,
In case there might be a blow-up with petrol getting red hot by the
    second,
Trying to stop it.
The ambulance crew were everywhere,
With the lorry,
The rest were with the firemen helping the crew,
Ambulances coming to and from the scene,
Taking the passengers to nearby hospitals.
There will be a few drivers, passengers, or families killed.
Now there is a helicopter at the scene to help.
It will take hours to clear this nasty accident,
All because of one lorry.
Surely with more space and less speed,
Probably, there wouldn't have been such a pile-up.

The crew kept going no matter what.
Seen enough, slowly moving on from the scene.
Heard on the news about the accident,
Five killed.
The lorry driver had a heart attack,
Didn't say whether he is still alive or not.
It took ten hours to clear the motorway.
Just then I thought about the police telling the families their loved ones
    had been in an accident.
The next day, I walked across the footbridge and looked over to where the
    accident took place.
I was amazed to see the motorway was back to normal as if nothing had
    happened,
Except I knew different,
I was watching it from the start.

3rd September 2014

Getting Ready to Go to Lourdes

“This poem and the next few, up to 'Looking Back', were written when I came home from the trip to Lourdes with the Disabled Catholic ”

Fellowship in June 2014.
A meeting is laid on for us
To get information about pick-ups
And many other bits and pieces,
All important points to remember.
Feeling tense and nervous,
Feeling the odd one out by my disabilities,
Wondering about my care,
Wondering what they are going to be like,
With John beside me to assure me
That everything will be all right.
A nurse came over and introduced herself to me,
Her name is Olivia and she sounds friendly enough,
John thinks that we will get on well after a few days,
I think so too, but it is still nerve-racking.
I know that some nurses are very particular
In the way they look after some people.
I'm sure Olivia and I will make the most of our time
With chatting, fun, laughing and caring;
Getting to know each other and working together
Is the most important part of the Lourdes trip.
I'm not sure about the second nurse
As we only said, 'Hello.'
I know I will have Richard to fall back on.
After all, Richard has been learning how to handle me.

29th May 2014

STARTING OUT

Up at 4am,
Quick wash, dressed,
Had my medication,
Ate half of a Rice Krispies bar.
5.30am, wrong car came.
Screaming, shouting, yelling
At John, but he lifted me in, in the end,
With the driver's help.
Arrived at pick-up place,
Yelling, shouting, screaming,
Hurting my foot, back and arms.
John made it with a big struggle.
Realised wheelchair bag was at home;
Tony and John went back to collect my bag.
Getting me on the coach was easy,
Collected Tony and my bag, then on our way.
At the airport, no delays, no problems,
Getting me in and off the plane,
Everything went smoothly.

Arrived at Hosanna House,
Feeling nervous, remembering
I can rely on Richard at any time when needed.
Had refreshments but were fatty,
Then shown to our rooms, pleased with mine,
Fantastic, two beds by the window and one opposite,
Me, opposite the window, facing it, which I like,
Especially in the morning when I wake up
To see a little bit of light shining through.
Now, I am completely dependent on others for care,
Nothing is like being at home as I know how I cope.
What I can do is to work together as a team.
In my eyes, enjoy being waited on!
Having chats, fun and laughter.
Now we are on our pilgrimage journey.
Took me three days to say Jalia and five days to say Goretti.

17th June 2014

FOOD, WORSHIP AND PARTIES

You could say I am a fusspot,
Don't like this or that,
Don't like greasy or spicy food,
Eat a bit of it, then it turns my belly over.
There are days when I can get away with it,
And other days I can't – then I'm sick.
In Lourdes I put Richard in charge of what I wanted.
Three meals a day is just too much for me.
Ate loads of French bread, which I loved,
Don't eat a lot of bread at home,
Lovely crusty bread with loads of butter and jam.
They would get me to try a bit of this or the other.
Most times when Richard got my food,
There was something else in it;
That wasn't Richard's fault but the kitchen staff's.
The best one was a plain banana sandwich.

I can't always join the worship;
Depends on where it is being held.
Old buildings or churches can be a nuisance,
Vibration, darkness, can't get close to the priest to hear.
Hosanna House was fine, could hear mostly everything.
Singing hymns can be a problem as I can't see the words,
Been blind since year 2000.
Singing old worship songs – lovely if I knew the words;
When I didn't I would go into my own worship.

To be honest I don't really like parties – that's why I drink,
To relax, calm me and to let go, to join in.
There will never be another person like Mark,
Who I met on the Jumbulance trip to Lourdes in 2009.
We were at a party and the music was going,
Mark came over and pulled me into the dancing area,
Took my footplates round the side of the wheelchair,
Lifted me forward a bit, then he got down onto his knee.
We put our arms round and holding each other,
Rocking side to side with a song playing,
It was such a lovely feeling of being wanted.
We stayed there till two or three songs went by,
Then we went into a corner just chatting away.
I have been back to Lourdes five times.
At every party I will always think of Mark
As there will never be another person like him.

3rd July 2014

A Day on the Lake

A lovely sunny hot day.
Visited a lake at the bottom of a mountain,
Which was on my left with trees in the background.
When the sun shone through the water
That came down from the mountain,
It gave me the optical illusion of a rainbow.
The wind blew very softly and not a leaf moved.
I could see the mountain with snow on top,
Which made me feel cold for a second.
Can see the mountaintop more closely outside Hosanna House,
A restaurant on my right.
Just sitting there watching the water,
Hearing the sound as it flows down,
As the water washes against the stones,
Rainbow colours on the water from the sun,
Can be so peaceful at times.
Another area for rowing and motor boats.
Wondering if I could get in one;
I would love to have a go.
To my amazement Tony and Richard did manage.
It was a lovely feeling being taken for a ride.
Had to keep very still as I was on the right, not the left,
As I could have put my left hand in the water;
Maybe it was just as well as I could get up to mischief.
I was happy as I didn't think it was possible.
Slowly, my time was coming up to get off
And back into my wheelchair.
How relaxing that ride felt to me.
Where there is a will, there is a way.

5th July 2014

Coming Home

As the final night was passing by,
At our final party, which was fun,
It was really late, a thunderstorm.
Father Jim was singing as I went outside;
I love the Irish music and the Irish songs.
Watched the lightning going across the sky,
See as far as the mountaintop,
The lightning was behind the mountain.
Got pulled by Julie-Anne to stay;
Olivia was pulling me to go to bed
As it had gone well over midnight.
They don't know what time I go to bed,
When I'm at home any time after 1am,
I can be a late or an early bird.
So cool and lovely outside, wanted to stay,
I could stay all night.
Had no choice but to do as I was told.

Jalia and her cousin did my packing,
They were just like Jo.
Didn't have to worry about anything,
Felt like a queen,
Waited on from hand to foot.
Cases had to be outside our room by 8am,
Including the bedding for the cleaners to wash.
Had our final service – didn't know many songs.
Went outside to take a last look at the mountain,
Thinking that in ten hours' time I'll be back home.
Flight went really well, pick-up coach from airport.
Well, Tony and Richard couldn't get me in,
Gangway in coach too small, OK if I could walk.
Richard and I came home by cab, the luxury way,
But poor Tony, not only paid for the cab,
Had to bring our cases round in his own car.
Members go home, jolly, happy, laughing,
Nurses and helpers go home feeling tired and exhausted,
But it's been worth every minute of their time.

8th July 2014

Looking Back

Looking back over the holiday,
I enjoyed it better than I thought I would.
What fun and laughter I had
With these people around me,
Especially at mealtimes and in my room.
After a couple of days,
My bad experiences of the past trips had disappeared.
I was glad I didn't have a nurse sharing my room,
As I tend to worry myself for nothing.
The hot weather made all the difference.
I wish I had a bit more time on my own,
So that I could sing and meditate on God
Without feeling shy or nervous.
I don't really like dancing,
Unless I'm doing it in style.
I did like the fancy dress do this year.
I didn't take anything with me,
Like I had done before.
The girls enjoyed dressing me up,
Certainly made a good job of it,
An Indian.
I missed Don and Jerry,
The helpers who couldn't come,
As they had other commitments.
Every now and then I would think about them.
Here and there I did manage to close my eyes, to praise God under my breath.
I usually ask people questions about their faith.
I didn't know whether to go to confession or not
Because I know I can go to Jesus to confess.
This year has been the best
Out of the three times I went with DCF!
Overall the helpers managed to look after me,
Despite my disability!

16th October 2014

Nothing

How could something come from nothing?
Out of nothing.
This is about nothing,
It is not about something.
Nothing is nothing.
You cannot say anything about nothing
Because nothing is nothing.
How could something come from nothing?
How did everything come from nothing?
If all came from nothing.

What can I say about nought?
Is it just another word for nothing, as zero?
I find it easier to say nought than zero.

Zero means nothing as well as nought does.
We say zero is used more than nought,
Making sure the scales are on zero,
Passing card numbers over the phone we use zero,
In maths, we tend to use zero whenever.
Zeros can have as many noughts as they like,
But it still means nothing.

Nil means nothing too,
But is used in a different way,
Mostly in sports like football and rugby.
Sometimes nil is for filling in forms.
It is a handy little word for Scrabble.
There are other words that mean NOTHING.

You are born with nothing,
You die with nothing,
But we can't say there was nothing created in the beginning
Because God was here when nothing was on earth!

17th November 2014

Computering

Mum had a typewriter.
In my younger days,
I did use it when I wanted to.
Charlton Park School,
Used a Possum machine,
Was very confusing to learn,
And an IBM electric typewriter.
Using a computer never entered my mind.
My brother-in-law Andy
Kept saying to me in the early eighties,
'You don't know what you are missing
And what you can do on a computer.
It will save you time and energy.
No more Tipp-Ex paper for correcting.'
Dad and I went and bought a Spectrum,
I was very pleased with it.
Andy said, 'No! That's not what I meant!'
Bought a new computer after a year,
Wow! Couldn't believe it – how true it is.
Went to college to learn more,
Word-processing, database, spreadsheet etc.,
Never-ending learning computering!
Packed it up for a while as I had gone blind,
On to *SuperNova* software, now using *Guide*.
Wow, can use a computer again.
How happy I am for that and so much more!

RISK

Risk, how far back does it go?
As far back as the Garden of Eden.
Where does the word come from?

It doesn't matter where you start in life,
As it is part of life and a vicious circle.
Life can be full of risk-taking,
There will always be a risk somewhere,
From the time you are born, until you die,
During pregnancy and up till that child reaches eighteen
Under the parents' care can still be risky,
Wondering whether you have made the right choice.

When we are grown up and have our own mind,
Life can become more risk-taking as there are so many different journeys.
Some paths have more risks than others,
But we always have to make that choice.

My Three Male PAs

Tim woke me up.
Before I was fully awake,
Took me a few minutes to realise
He can go on about something.
Oh, Tim, for God's sake, let me get up.
Can jump to the wrong conclusion,
But will always apologise afterwards.
Can repeat himself from time to time,
I just say, 'Stop,' and he stops.
Always does his best for me.
But it is his gentleness that I like,
And his calmness which comes with it!

Wayne, on the other hand,
Is such a quick dash,
Heavy-handed at times.
Does have a reason for this,
But why always in a hurry?
At least that's what it feels like to me.
Can hurt me from time to time,
Won't believe me when I tell him.
Pushing me when on the streets
Can make me feel sick.
He can go much too fast,
Can't slow him down in any way.
Upsets me from time to time.
He's just a quick dash,
But can't be changed in any way.
Oh! How much I wish I could slow him down!

John, a close friend, later my carer,
Hears all my frustrations,
Often gets it in the neck from me,
Moan, groan and whatever.
Used to wind me up and succeed,
Now, he doesn't always.
Where would I be without him?
Depend on him for so much,
No matter what that might be.

To me it feels like a vicious circle.
Tim and Wayne get moans and picked on,
On those days, just want to be left alone,
Can't as I always need help somewhere.
How I wish I could just get up without being
    pulled this way or that way.
They think they know all the answers!
'Oh, your foot moved, it's not where I put it.'
This makes me feel I want to scream.

Tim and Wayne go home when finished.
John doesn't as he is always here for me!

HOIST (2)

Had a new hoist delivered,
Supposed to hold me better.
Neil came to demonstrate with another Jo.
Felt left out when they were laughing.
I called my Jo to explain what was going on,
So I could laugh with them,
Then it was my turn to try it out.
I like it, but not the *harness*.
I promised Neil that I will give it a go.
I believe he liked my poems about the first hoist.
The one about Neil made him nervous.
He realised it was nothing bad, but good.
When he hugged me I don't know why I didn't hug him back.
I do love being hugged as it can mean so many things,
Appreciation, pleasure, thankfulness, friendship.

I knew I wouldn't have time to go to the loo in the new hoist.
I made Jo take me off the loo using the hoist.
It felt really OK and better for my legs.
Tim makes me nervous when he uses the hoist.
The harness does hurt my arms, neck and shoulders.
Don't like being lifted in the sitting position,
Feel I'm not in control with my legs.
He does moan and get on my nerves about it.
Fun when Jo and I show Wayne how to do it.
Wayne tied the leg bit around my wheelchair,

A good job that Wayne didn't lift me up.
We laughed and saw the funny side of it.
Will only use it when I tell him to.
John won't use it, wouldn't give it a go,
Yet I can understand why – an accident,
Slid right through the harness, couldn't get up,
Needed an extra pair of hands to help,
Tim, just left, phoned to call him back;
Between them, they managed to lift me.
I grew to like it, but *not* the bloody harness,
Will try a new one when I return from Tenerife.
Doesn't give me much time as we start all over again.

18th June 2014

Hoist (3)

Second hoist is slightly different,
Wider at the top and narrower at the bottom.
This does make it difficult for my right arm.
Straps go round each leg to support me standing.
After the demo, Jo was the first to use it.
I thought, *Blimey, this will take even longer.*
What about when in an emergency?
Bad enough with the first hoist.
Tim turned up the next morning, hurting me with the harness,
Doesn't matter how much we tried to make it comfortable.
Worse time is when I'm in my nightie.

Jo and I decided to hire a hoist when in Tenerife.
All thanks to Neil, it arrived in our room in the hotel.
To our amazement it was the same hoist which I had been given by Neil to
    try out the last few weeks at home.
The only thing it didn't have was a strap.
This pleased Jo, and I was happy with it.
Jo said it didn't matter as strap doesn't really do anything.
Like being held in the standing-up position.
How am I going to tell Tim when I get home?
Used the hoist more and more as the holiday went by.
It would support me when on the loo;
I had nothing to hold on to – no hand rails.
We trained Edna to use it, what fun we had with it,
Was it because Jo and Edna could move much quicker?
We bumped into things – the wall and the toilet.

At one point, sitting on the loo I took a good look and saw,
The top handles reminded me of the *South Bank Show* symbol
Where the electric light goes from finger to finger,
My handles are wider apart, like a motorbike,
The hook bar is like a punch bag as I bang my head on it,
The bits I get my thumbs caught on could be the indicator,
Where my feet go are the pedals,
Whatever I'm sitting on is a motorbike seat.

The harness is like being in any prison in the old days,
Like a form of punishment,
The longer you are in it, the more it hurts your neck, shoulder and arm.

Apart from the last stanza, there is nothing you can do about the bloody
    harness.
I've just got to put up with it.
In Tenerife the harness was tighter and older,
So it didn't bloody hurt me quite so much as the one I've got now!
Next week we have got to start all over again with a new one.

Carole brought around a harness from her office.
At last it is the right one for me,
After all the palaver.

2nd July 2014

MONDAY-TO-MONDAY (2)

"The original Monday-to-Monday, in Chapter One, was written in 1973."

This version was written in 2015.
Monday, back to work
Unless it's a bank holiday.
Tuesday, doing my best,
So many hours in a day.
Wednesday, tired, feeling 'ergh',
Trying to keep the work up,
Getting bored and fed up.
Thursday, need a holiday
To get away from it all.
Friday, weekend is starting,
A break from work or whatever.
Saturday, shopping, housework,
Doing other bits and pieces.
Sunday, going to church,
Relaxing with family or friends.
Monday, here again, back to work.
Where does the time go?
Start all over again!

OCCUPATIONAL THERAPIST (2)

Scared, nervous, worried,
Carol instead of Neil, oh well.
What is going to happen this time?
Wayne was here instead of Jo.
Meeting started off well,
Slowly moving on to using the hoist,
I thought, *Ooh-err, here we go!*
Carol did say about handling me using the hoist.
Even though I know she is right,
We all know about the harness;
That one, we will never get right!
Demonstrate getting me in and out of the bed.
John and Tim are tall, Jo and Wayne are shorter,
Tim always uses the hoist but John does when necessary.
Carol noticed that John was doing more harm to himself and his back.
Carol got frightened as John rolled me onto my side.
Mind you, we were using the slip mat!
Did she really think I would roll off the bed?
John certainly got a warning, but was right!
Suggested getting a hospital bed,
Thought rushing through my mind,
No, no, not that, too big, too long and too wide,
How are we going to get two beds in my bedroom?
OK, OK, I'll give it a go, but I'm warning you!
If I don't like the bed, back it goes.
On the day of it arriving,

Had to alter the bedroom around a bit.
Wayne managed to change it around in an hour.
Saw the bed and didn't know what to think.
Got in it the first night,
Took ages to sleep,
Couldn't move my bum over but getting there.
Next night, too tired, slept well, no pain.
Bed not going back, John gets my other bed.
Pepper, my cat, like both beds
For her own use, my bed for the window!
John's bed for the warmth and to sleep!
Now, back to the harness again!
Not looking forward to that.
What a palaver that is going to be!

5th March 2015

"*In September 2015, the occupational therapist Carol again came to see me. I told her how much I thought she had changed, for the better. Then she told me that she was not the same Carol. There were two OTs with the same name.*"

24/11/2015

Eltham or Woolwich

I went to Waterfront Sports Centre.
How much has changed since 2004.
Could hardly do anything there now.
A few machines I used to go on.
I was pleased to see one machine there;
I used to be quite good on it,
But could cut the edge of my wrist
While holding and cycling with my arms.
Wayne and John tried to help me on,
My body, right arm and hand wouldn't let me do it!
Had to hide my true feeling,
Felt like crying and could not speak for a while.
All the exercises I'm doing at Eltham are a waste!
John and Wayne assure me it is not a waste of time.
I wonder how far I would have got if I hadn't left when I did!
Over time things change, as well as my body getting older.
At Eltham, there is so much more that I can do.
Looking at it from that angle, I feel a great deal better!
It's just that the Waterfront is closer to home than *Eltham*!

19th April 2015

Professionals

Professionals,
Whatever field they work in,
Some I like more than others;
Depends on what it's all about.
I can be very anxious beforehand,
Wondering what he or she is going to say.
After the visitor has said their part,
I hope that person will see where I'm coming from.
Care managers, Social Services and the council
Are very good and helpful.
Some are very conscientious at their job.
Only one that really scares me,
Which is the occupational therapist!
I know this person means well and is doing their best,
But he or she makes me feel worse,
Especially over the hoist and the harness!
It can be very demanding at times.
I should be able to stand firm and not give in.
Over the last few years, there were times when I had to.
The OT has a duty to look after my PAs as well as me.
All my PAs have their own way of using the hoist
But in the end, it should be me to decide.
If I'm comfortable with the way the carer is lifting,
Then I am happy to continue to do so!
I do get bad days just like other disabled people,
And my PAs get bad days too!
I am so pleased when the OT says, 'I'll see you in six months' time.'

23rd April 2015

CATHOLIC CHURCH IN LEWISHAM

This is a Catholic Church
In Lewisham High Street.
I don't know how old it is.
Before 1998, I would pop in.
How quiet it is once inside,
Away from the noise and traffic.
There were always little booklets on show;
I did buy some for my own interest,
And put the money in a small slot.
For my quiet time, praying,
Sometimes I could smell the incense,
Which I like so much,
Made it feel extra special.
If no one was there,
I would sing out quietly.
I would take a look at Jesus,
When they took him off the cross.
I didn't like that figure, so I hurried on
To the next statue, which is Mary.
I could kneel or stand there for a time,
Then move on to the crucifix.
There I would kneel down and pray,
In this part of the church, especially.
At Easter – cover the crucifix
With flowers around the surface.
At Christmas – a beautiful nativity,

A stable, Mary, Joseph,
Baby Jesus in a manger,
Animals, shepherds.
A lady may be in the repository;
We would have a general chat,
If she wasn't busy.
A few Sundays,
I would attend their service,
Amazed to see the church full,
Couldn't sit down anywhere,
Then I managed to squeeze myself in.
There was one thing I really did hate!
When I pop in to say a prayer or two,
In front of the altar – a coffin!
I daren't go near it or pass it,
The thought of a dead body
Gives me the creeps and out I go!
Go back in a couple of days later,
There won't be another coffin for a while!
I could enjoy my quiet time again!
I do miss visiting it nowadays.

27th April 2015

King's Church (2)

Thinking about King's Church.
Too far from here to Catford.
Told about King's at Lee,
Wow, great news, hang on a sec,
Thoughts are rushing through,
Not from the past but me now.
How would I react now?
Have to take a PA with me,
More disabled, more dependent,
Don't want to act like a dummy,
Want to do some wheelchair dancing,
But need to organise it with Gill,
Not just being a church member.
Shall I go and try it out?
On my first visit met Pat B there,
Liked what I saw and heard, a friendly bunch.
To my amazement Wayne enjoyed it too.
John said, 'You have enough hours.'
Ask Wayne if he could work it,
Wondering how King's Church will respond.
Will they see me as an equal?
What am I looking for in the church?
I don't want Wayne to do the answering for me,
Unless I know that a member doesn't understand me,
Then Wayne has every right to repeat what I said.
This Sunday will be my twelfth week!
Knowing what I really want,
Trying to find a way to listen to the sermons
At home by using *Guide* software,
Not having much success but getting there!
I can't commit myself to joining,
I don't know what support I will get.
Will they come and collect me?
Will they help me to join a group?

Will they get me a coffee – or hold it for me?
Will someone be able to take me to the loo?
The church is having a barbecue – can I go?
When my PA can't work or goes sick,
King's Church holds get-together evenings,
But could I go? I would really love to.
I'm not going to impose myself onto anyone.
If the church can't meet these requirements,
Then King's Church is not ready for people like me!
Then how can I join with all these questions?
But I do like going there,
Want them to see me as a person!

3rd May 2015

" *Mark G finally managed to email the sermons to me. Started going to 'Bring and Share' group. Still got a long way to go in accepting people with disabilities.* "

Fireworks

Wow! It's fireworks here once again.
I used to love watching my dad
Starting the bonfire off,
Then getting the fireworks ready
By putting them into a tin.
Mum, Linda and I would go out
Into the garden to watch Dad light
The fireworks one by one,
Whoosh, bang and exploding into colours,
Beautiful red, pink, yellow and others,
Different colour red dying down into pink,
Then Dad would fix a Catherine wheel onto a fence,
Then we would watch the wheel go round and round,
Throwing different colours into the surrounding areas.
I didn't like the Jumping Jack,
We never knew where it would jump to,
Then it would make us jump too!
Some were too big for your eyes to see.
We would say, 'Wow, did you see that?'
One of us would have replied, 'Yes, and all the colours sprinkled into the
    surrounding area.'
When Dad had lit all the fireworks,
He gave us some sparklers to hold.
When lit they would sparkle into little round stars.
While Dad was keeping the bonfire under control,
Mum started getting the buffet ready,
Consisted of chestnuts and all other bits and pieces.
Mum, Linda and I started eating,
Waiting for Dad to come and join us,
Watching other neighbours' fireworks going off.
As the years roll on,
Less people have fireworks in their garden,
More people go to firework displays.

During the late eighties and onwards,
I would go to John's flat,
Stand outside on his balcony.
We could see for miles.
John would say, quick, look to the left or the right.
It was fantastic to see so many fireworks.
Where I'm living now and being blind,
I still like fireworks but don't know what colour I can see.
When John and I watch firework displays on TV,
I like them, but John has to tell me the colours,
The only colour I see is white.
As I watch the fireworks go off,
They are still fantastic!

23rd May 2015

16/12/2012

Catholic Church (2)

In the Catholic Church again,
When I used to pop in
For my prayer time,
I thought about something else.
Looking around the wall,
To my amazement,
I saw the story of Jesus dying,
All in little pictures,
Etched in the plaster wall.
I think it goes back to the days
When people couldn't read.
I made my way back to the cross,
Where the figure of Christ lay.
The colour is more yellow
Than a natural skin colour,
Browny red where the nails have been,
A mark where He was pierced.
Had a bit of time on my hands;
I wanted to watch some people,
To see what they do to the figure.
Some could kiss it or touch it,
Others would kiss their fingers,

Then place them on the figure.
Some would just stand and look down.
Wondering what is going through their mind,
Praying, confessing or thanking,
Thinking where I was standing,
I don't know what I thought.
It didn't really impress me much.
It sort of made me think.
As I was leaving the church,
I know what I will be saying now:
Thank you for dying on the cross,
Know that my sins are forgiven.
I know Jesus did die for you and me,
He gave us the gift of the Holy Spirit.
Sometimes I feel Jesus is far away,
But deep inside me, He is always at my side,
He will never leave me despite what I'm going through!

31st May 2015

ROSIE

Rosie, my cat, a feral kitten,
About three years old, a tabby,
Had a lovely ginger around her middle.
She was an indoor cat.
At first, she would go into hiding
Behind the TV; we couldn't get her out!
John was worried about the wires,
Rosie could get caught up in them.
Edna managed to get her out.
Edna says, 'If they can get in, they can get out!'
Rosie found another hiding place,
In a corner by the window in my bedroom,
Then behind the settee for ages.
Very, very slowly she began to come out,
We were able to make a fuss over her.
Whoever came to visit me,
She would just look and go back.
Rosie liked her butterfly toy the best,
And would have her mad half-an-hour, as they call it.
She would hate going to the vet – but good once there.
When the vet finished checking her over,
She would jump back into her basket!
As time went by she got on my lap more and more,
And would love her tummy rubbed.
What a cat she turned out to be.
She started to sleep on the bed,
Then one day I woke up to find her snuggled up
    under my duvet asleep with her head on my pillow!

2nd June 2015

"In March 2013, Rosie wasn't well. After blood tests the vet told us that her kidneys were failing. He explained that though she was unwell she wasn't in pain. There was no cure and as it progressed it would cause her pain. John, Jo and I agreed it was better to have Rosie put to sleep while she was happy. The vet agreed with our decision. I had Rosie on my lap while she passed away."

15/02/2012

ON THE ROAD

Don't like these,
Don't like me either,
Dial-a-Ride,
Can't always be booked when needed,
Seat belt – too high up on my neck,
Can choke me when braking.
Some drive too fast – go flying forward,
Turning left – body goes over to the right,
Jump up off my seat over these sleeping policemen.
Some drivers are caring, others are not,
Can make me feel sick.
Not always reliable – can be a nuisance,
Complaining – *why*, when I don't pay!

Black cabs,
The same as above,
Worse on most journeys.
No seat belt – bend at all angles,
Wheelchair can't keep still,
Can bang my head on the window.
Watch out! When caught in traffic,
Time is racing on – clock ticking away,
Can add more to my cost.
That is how these cabs make their money!

Four-by-four or people carrier,
I hate these cars,
Seat too high,
Me, too short to climb in.

I like going on buses.
The ramp comes out, on I get,
By the window I stay,
Body gets moved about a bit,
Turn my face to sunbathe,
Tell the driver our bus stop,
Out comes the ramp – off we get.
A nuisance from time to time,
Can't get on – full with pushchairs!
Just doesn't stop – wait for the next bus.
That's all right when not in a rush!

Put me in a car – I will love it,
Doesn't matter how far we go,
Just like the feel from the engine,
Sound from the rain falling on the car roof!
When windows open – other cars rushing by,
When windy, sounds like thunder in my ears.
Feel sad – journey ends here or there.

15th June 2015

HAIRDRESSER

Sixtieth birthday coming up,
Wanted my hair done,
Colour, wash, cut and blow dry.
Didn't know where to go.
Went to Woolwich with Jo,
Two salons close to each other.
Jo and I went into one salon,
While waiting to be served
Just looking around to see how we felt,
Didn't like the atmosphere,
Looked at each other – out we went,
To the next salon, a few doors away.

Once inside, liked what we saw,
Knew this was the one for me,
Felt comfortable, a friendly bunch.
Introduced to Nicky – going to do my hair.
The way I got treated, hair colour,
Wash, head massage, cut and blow dry,
Never felt like this in any salon.
Nicky wasn't in a hurry to get my hair done,
When finished, asked Jo for her approval.
Nicky won Jo's approval, which pleased me.

About three years on,
I'm still going there for my hairdo,
Get offered tea, coffee or water.
Just a tidy-up, this time by Nicky,
Had the usual treatment.
Knows where my parting goes;
Others had their own ideas.
When finished – before paying,
Nicky bent down to my level,
Told me that she is leaving.
A lump came up in my throat.
Cheered me up by saying
The same company,
Their salon in Eltham High Street.
I am so pleased about this.
I looked at Jo and said, 'Can I?'
Nicky has her reason for the move.
She hugged me, kissed me on my cheek.
I paid the bill and said goodbye,
Asked Jo when outside the salon.
Jo answered, 'I think we can,'
So here I come, Nicky,
To your new working place!

28th June 2015

John Ryan, I Remember ...

"My friend Gill C visited me on Tuesday 25th August and suggested that I could write a poem about John to be read out at the crematorium on Friday 28th August. Over the weekend I added one or two verses to it to make it sound better. Gill corrected my English."

I remember when you started working at Ladywell in the eighties,
I thought ... *You look down in the dumps!*
I felt concerned about you, but I did not know why.
I plucked up courage to ask you what the matter was.
You wouldn't tell me, but you asked me out instead!
You shared with me your worries and I felt empathy towards you.
I remember asking you to come to the European Parliament
    in Brussels,
And I was shocked when you agreed!
From then on you were my companion.
I remember how intelligent you were.
All those questions I used to ask you
About history, religion, politics and more.
You made it all so much more interesting,
Especially when we visited historical places or castles.
I remember the tricks you loved to play on me,
The names you used to call me!
And how it annoyed you when I called you 'Darling';
You hated that.
And I soon learnt never to dare you
Because you couldn't resist a dare!
I remember, as the years went by,
How you really cared for me
And I for you, though in a different way.
I thank you for all the love and care
That you gave to me.
I remember the arguments we had over Jesus

And you had with the people at the centre.
So when I sat down with you
As you underwent treatment for cancer,
I was amazed by the faith that you did have.
I remember the fun we had with Jo and Edna
On holidays together.
But slowly, John, you became ill
And our friendship deepened.
Then Rosie the cat came along 'out of the blue'
And you grew to love her, as I did.
I remember as you became more weary
And often slept on my bed,
You never minded when I woke you for your help.
I remember the last time I visited you in hospital
I wanted to get closer to you, to be alone.
I'll never forget the way you looked at me.
I wanted to put my arms around you, but couldn't.
I will always remember the last kiss you gave me
And how hard it was for you to reach me.
John, you will always be in my heart.
I long to feel your presence again
And will always treasure saying goodbye to you
In the Chapel of Rest, until we meet again in Heaven.

25th–31st August 2015

Conclusion

John and I have been part of a Catholic church since 2009. I really feel it is not for me as I don't believe everything in the Catholic faith. I would like to think it is for John as he is an active member. When I do go I do get a good 'Hello', and especially from Father Jim. I do go to the monthly disabled Catholic service.

I honestly believe God used me and my friend Gill to help John find the right church for him.

I'm happy spending time with God at home ...

The hardest thing for me is to learn to *trust* and *obey* God in everything I do in my life.

Nothing is impossible with God.

Luke 1:37

This verse has become my motto:

Treat other people as you would like them to treat you.

Jewish Bible, Luke 6:31

Never above you,
Never below you,
But always by your side.

Katie G. told me that when I was small. I still remember it today.

By Julia A. Mitchell
21st April 2014

Epilogue

Another year has gone by since I wrote the above. I would like to bring you up to date with a few things which have changed over the past fourteen months.

As John and I began to realise that our prayer list was getting longer, we decided to break our prayers over seven days.

Saturdays:	the Church
Sundays:	the world
Mondays:	our families
Tuesdays:	Pats night
Wednesdays:	anything
Thursdays:	PAs
Fridays:	the sick, pray for those in need

Sometimes these overlap with each other.

We will always end our prayer time with John saying the Hail Mary. We both say the Lord's Prayer, 'Glory Be to the Father' and 'Lord Jesus Christ', then I will finish it with, 'Grant me the patience to accept the things I cannot change, the courage to change the things I can and the wisdom to know the difference.'

Most evenings I will say a prayer for Pepper, my cat, that as time goes by she will get used to me and start coming up more and more.

In 2013, I didn't like going to St Joseph's Church in the winter as it can be very cold inside. So I stopped attending. I would listen to Premier Radio from 8am onwards. John would leave my place any time after 9am. Wayne used to leave me at 11am; I had a whole hour to myself! I could phone my friends, shout at God from time to time, and I would always go into the kitchen as there was a drink and some chocolates waiting for me! I went back to St Joseph's now and again.

In 2015, I got a bit fed up listening to Premier Radio. I felt like I wanted to try out King's Church at Lee.

As I was finishing this book, sadly John fell over and cut his head open and was taken to hospital. During the weeks he was in hospital, God told me that he was ready to take John and He was just waiting for John, and I replied, 'OK, Lord – I will let him go. It will be very hard for me but I will let him go.' But I didn't say anything to John about this.

Whilst he was in hospital, John wasn't eating anything and I began to realise that because of this he wasn't keeping his strength up. He asked Jo and me to do him a favour – to get some cash out for him and take it in to him. This was on 21st July. As John was having his dialysis session, I made Jo go in to give him the cash and I waited outside, and Jo kissed him goodbye.

On 22nd July, Wayne took me in to see John early in the evening, and we stayed there for a while. Then, just before we left, I asked John to kiss me goodbye and it was such an effort for John to lean over to give me that kiss, but we made it. I couldn't get my arm around him because my wheelchair wouldn't get up close enough to the bed. The way John kissed me was different from the normal way he would kiss me.

When Wayne and I came out of the ward, I wanted to go back, but in my mind I thought Wayne wouldn't take me back. Then at 3.45am on Thursday 23rd July 2015, John passed away.

I believe the hospital did try to ring me and I thought it was my community alarm so I didn't take it. So it was Georgie Fox who told me later on that morning that John had passed away.

Believe me, John did look after me as long as he could. We had planned to go away to Southampton so that I could have a day trip on a Jubilee Trust ship, and John rang up Georgie and asked her to take his place. Georgie was very happy to do it for him so I could get my day trip on the boat.

Big Changes

My life is turned upside down once again.
How am I going to cope without you, John?
Nothing is going to be the same again.
Everything is changing for the worse.
Things I won't be able to do any more.

God told me that He was ready for you, John,
And that I will be all right.
Who am I going to look up to now?
John, you used to do everything concerning me.
Yes, I knew who that person was.
There was so much to do
Sorting out all of your stuff, John.

We usually went to bed well past midnight,
Except when I was not well.
It can take a long time to settle,
Let alone go to sleep!
Now I'm put to bed by 10 or 10.30pm.
I have no choice over this
But to do what I'm told – like a little girl!
I'm just not used to it.

I stare into space wondering,
Until I drop off to sleep.
It's my PAs putting me to bed, not you, John.
PAs have to get home.
John, you stayed at my place and
It made all the difference
Going to bed when we finished our jobs.

When I wake up at five or earlier,
Turning over on my back
After lying on my side for nine hours or more,
I can't get up.
It drives me crazy, John,
I feel so useless.
It makes me mad just lying there,
All the things I could do if I was up.

I just think, pray or let my mind wander off.
I tell God what I think – but I'm not praying.
I feel so frustrated waiting for my PA.
John, you were there when I needed you.
You would put my hearing aids in,
To listen to UCB radio's breakfast show.
John, I can't listen to that properly now.
You were such a good carer.

Pepper, my cat, doesn't always help either.
Going to bed, she could bite my hand!
She will sleep above my pillow and
In the morning when I need her
To comfort me she does, but
Only when it suits her.
She can be lovely,
But not when she bites!
I keep hoping she will change in time.

I suddenly realise just how much you did for me
And how much I miss you being around.
It is true what people say,
You do get used to it,
But it is not the same without you, John.
But God is helping me to cope.

5th November 2015

COPING WITHOUT JOHN

John, I know what I've got to do now
Is to find someone to trust to take over some of the jobs
Which you used to do for me.
John, I know you trusted Jo,
So Jo will be who I rely on.
John, I know you will be pleased,
As we have spoken about this in the past.

John, Christmas and New Year
Will never be the same again.
All the nice CDs you brought me,
All the fun and laughter we had,
Just you and me being alone.

John, I know Jo will do her best for me.
So will some of my other friends.
I know you are beside me,
Helping me to get through it.
And God is too.
John, I will always keep you in my mind,
Whatever the future holds for me.

9th November 2015

www.ingramcontent.com/pod-product-compliance
Lightning Source LLC
Chambersburg PA
CBHW032000040426

42448CB00006B/430